ELTON JOHN VISUAL DOCUMENTARY
BY NIGEL GOODALL

Edited by Chris Charlesworth
Cover & Book designed by 4i Limited
Picture research by David Brolan

ISBN: 0.7119.3078.3
Order No: OP 47028

Exclusive distributors:
Book Sales Limited,
8/9 Frith Street,
London W1V 5TZ, UK.

Music Sales Corporation,
225 Park Avenue South,
New York, NY 10003, USA.

Music Sales Pty Ltd,
120 Rothschild Avenue,
Rosebery, NSW 2018, Australia.

To the Music Trade only:
Music Sales Limited,
8/9 Frith Street,
London W1V 5TZ, UK.

Photo credits:
Front cover: Adrian Boot/Retna;
Bob Alford/Retna: 40br; Greg Allen/Retna: 90;
Adrian Boot/Retna: 3, 87; Alan
Davidson/Retna: 89; Dave Ellis/Redferns: 13t,
14b, 44tc; Famous: 61, 69tl&r, 104b; Bob
Gruen/Pictorial Press: 35; Mick
Hutson/Redferns: 86, 101t&c; Robin
Kaplan/Retna: 67br; Bob King: 40cr, 41b&tr,
66b; London Features International: 1, 4, 5, 10,
11t, 12, 15, 18t, 24, 27, 28l&r, 30t, 34t, 38, 40r,
41tl, 43t, 44bl, 44/45, 46, 49, 50, 52tl, 53tl&b,
54, 56, 57t&b, 58t&b, 62, 65, 67bl, 70t bl&br,
71t, 72, 74, 75, 76t&b, 77, 78, 79t&b, 80t, 81,
82, 83b, 84, 85c&b, 86c&b, 88, 91, 92, 93, 94,
95, 96, 97, 98, 100, 101b, 102, 103, 105, 106,
112; Ross Marino/Retna: 40cl; Pictorial Press:
6, 7, 31, 40tc, 48, 67t, 73; David Plastic/Retna:
69b; Barry Plummer: 18bl&br, 19t, 20r,
21tl&r, 22t&b, 25, 26t&b, 29, 30b, 32, 33c, 36,
42t&b, 43b, 44l, 45b, 47, 51, 52tr&b, 55t&b,
64, 68b, 70c, 71c&b; Michael Putland/Retna:
33b, 39, 43c, 45t, 53tr, 59, 60; David
Redfern/Redferns: 19b, 20l, 21b, 37; Tony
Russell/Redferns: 11b; Peter
Sanders/Redferns: 14t, 16, 33t; Barry
Wentzell/Pictorial Press: 23; Val
Wilmer/Redferns: 9; Vinnie Zuffante/Pictorial
Press: 85t.

Printed and bound in Singapore.

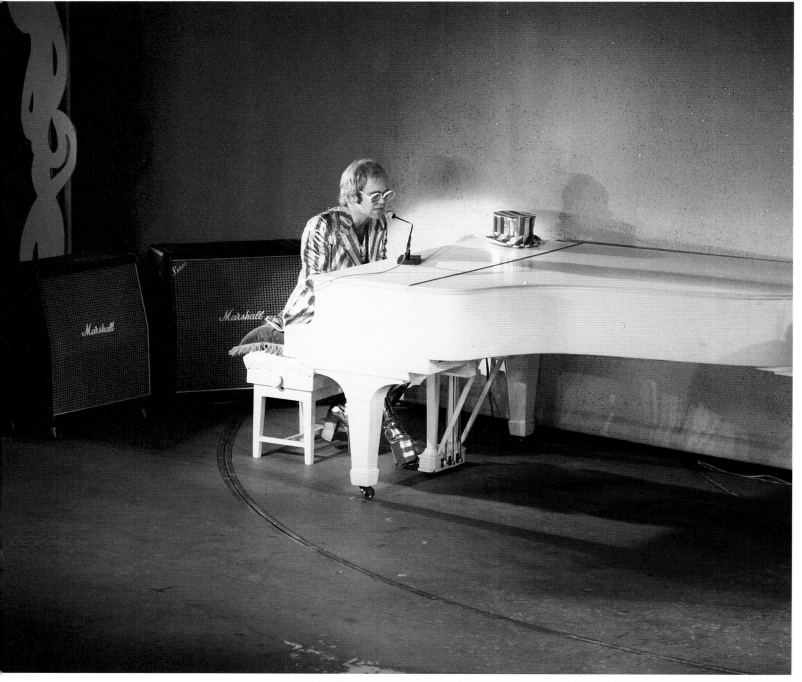

ELTON ON STAGE DURING THE ROYAL VARIETY PERFORMANCE AT THE LONDON PALLADIUM, OCTOBER 30, 1972

PREFACE & AUTHOR'S ACKNOWLEDGEMENTS

When Elton John and Bernie Taupin signed a new publishing deal with Time Warner late last year, the Chief Executive of Warner Chappell Music, Les Bider, commented that they were the Gershwins of their era. It was no small compliment to the man who began his career singing standards and passing the hat around in the Northwood Hills pub in Pinner, and who is now recognised not only as the UK's most consistently successful singer/songwriter but also as one of the most successful composers of popular music of all time.

In the twenty-four years beginning with the release of 'Empty Sky' in 1969, Elton has recorded 24 albums of original material, including two doubles, and several live albums, and released countless compilations. This is in addition to scores of singles and manifold contributions to the work of others. He is untypical of his peers in many respects, but the most obvious is that he is a chronic over-achiever; it is unlikely that any artist in the field of popular music, successful or otherwise, will have averaged anything like one album of original material per year over a 20-year career. Elton, of course, has averaged more.

Elton's success on record has been complemented by his enormous popularity as a live performer. Increasingly eccentric and flamboyant during the Seventies, Elton was probably the first rock star to parody himself in the name of entertainment, and his abundant good humour won him many fans the world over. His advancing years have brought about a toning down of the outrageousness, and the spotlight now shines on his talent as a piano player which was often overlooked amid the glitter and frenzy of his early years. He was, and remains, a terrific pianist.

Elton's personality, his celebrity status, nowadays often transcends his music. His close involvement with Watford Football Club, his friendships with other celebrities, including even the Royal Family, and the details and indiscretions of his tempestuous personal life seem to be known to everyone. It's the price he has to pay for having amassed a personal fortune estimated at over £100 million.

Elton's career has been celebrated by a special boxed set entitled 'To Be Continued', and his songwriting partnership with Bernie Taupin by a special album of cover versions entitled 'Two Rooms'. Ever before his public, Elton commenced a new world tour at the end of May 1992 which coincided with the release of 'The One', his first studio album since 1989.

Elton John - A Visual Documentary is the first book to thoroughly chronicle this hectic career. It is a comprehensive run-down of each move Elton has made, from playing keyboards in Bluesology in the Sixties to headlining his own concerts at Wembley Stadium. I have attempted to list every gig Elton has performed, whether as a member of Bluesology, or as a solo performer, together with every other important moment in his life. There is also a full discography containing every single and album on which Elton has appeared, together with relevant chart information for the UK and US. To list Elton's chart successes world-wide would be too great an undertaking.

For their help in compiling this visual documentary, the author would like to thank Chris Charlesworth, Nigel Cutteridge, Christine Whitehead, Lois James, Keith Hayward, and Vivienne Singer.

Nigel Goodall, December 1992

ELTON AND BERNIE, 1992

INTRODUCTION

Elton John was born in Pinner, Middlesex on 25 March 1947, and christened Reginald Kenneth Dwight. His father, Stanley, served in the RAF and met and married dark-haired, petite Sheila Harris in January 1945, five months before the end of World War II.

Stanley and Sheila lived at first with her parents in Pinner Hill Road where Reg was born. Although Stanley had played in the Bob Miller Band, he was a military careerist, a Flight Lieutenant, and he was often absent overseas on RAF service. Elton has made no secret of the fact that he was suppressed by, and often petrified of, his father and that there was little love between them. The only source of common interest within the family seems to have been music, though Reg's dad sometimes took his son to watch Watford FC play at Vicarage Road.

Young Elton's childhood was fairly restricted. With his father away for much of the time, his early years were spent almost exclusively in the company of his mother and grandmother. He was encouraged to bang the keys on the family piano while his mother and grandmother busied themselves with everyday chores. By the time Elton was four he could play the 'Skater's Waltz'.

As Stanley and Sheila's relationship deteriorated, Reg retreated into a musical fantasy. One of the great loves in the Dwight household was the collection of big breakable 78 rpm records by the stars of the pre-rock'n'roll era, stars like Guy Mitchell, Frankie Laine, Rosemary Clooney, Kay Starr and Billy May. "My first favourite was Winifred Atwell... I was knocked out by her," he remembers. "Then my mother came home with two records 'ABC Boogie' by Bill Haley and 'Heartbreak Hotel' by Elvis Presley. I'll never forget that. One was on Brunswick and the other on HMV. I really freaked when I heard them, and I went on from there."

Elton's schooldays were spent at Pinner Wood Junior Primary and Reddiford School. By the time he started at Pinner County Grammar, Stanley and Sheila's failing marriage had led to separation. It was around this time that Elton won a scholarship to the Royal Academy of Music where he would study each Saturday morning for the next five years. He had very little aptitude for academic subjects; instead of studying he would stay at home playing records, or skip off to watch a game of football. After his parents divorced, Elton continued to live with his mother who always encouraged his musical ambitions. "He was being forced to play classics when he wanted to play popular tunes," she recalls. "It wasn't until he was 11 or 12 that I found him a new teacher who let him play pop tunes, and from that time on this was all he was interested in."

On 5 March 1965, just two weeks before Elton was due to take his GCE 'A' level in music, he left school to work as a messenger for Mills Music, a West End music publisher. At night he played piano in the bar of the Northwood Hills Hotel in Pinner. "I sang and played piano there every Friday, Saturday and Sunday for a whole year," he remembers. "And during that whole period, I don't think that I ever missed a gig. I used to sing Jim Reeves songs, Cliff Richard songs, anything that was popular - and also play things like 'Roll Out The Barrel', Cockney songs, 'When Irish Eyes Are Smiling'... you had to play 'When Irish Eyes Are Smiling' otherwise you'd get a pint of beer slung over you. Al Jolson songs were also very popular. I used to have a box which used to be passed around at the end of the evening. When I first started my residency, nobody used to go into the public bar but eventually people started to come in and, after a while, it was packed out every weekend. With the money people used to put in my box I was earning about £25 a week, which was great."

With the proceeds of the Northwood Hills Hotel residency Elton bought an electric piano which he played in his first group, The Corvettes, formed with Stuart Brown, a friend of his cousin. Named after a brand of shaving cream, they played at children's parties held in Scout huts and other neighbourhood get-togethers, but they disbanded after the novelty wore off, only to re-form a year later, renaming themselves Bluesology after a tune by French jazz guitarist Django Reinhardt. Their line-up now comprised Mick Inkpen on drums, Rex Bishop on bass, Stuart Brown on guitar and vocals and Elton on electric piano. Their initial repertoire centred on soul material.

"We played Jimmy Witherspoon numbers like 'Times Are Getting Tougher Than Tough' and 'When The Lights Go Out'," says Elton. "Our lead singer Stuart Brown was Jimmy Witherspoon crazy, so that's what we used to play. I can remember playing the South Harrow British Legion Hall when all these rockers rode right into the place on their motorbikes and said that if we didn't play rock'n'roll they'd smash our gear up. I was into that, because at the time all I really wanted to do was play like Jerry Lee Lewis or Little Richard."

By 1965 Bluesology were playing dates in London's clubland. They became one of a score of London-based bands to be signed to the Philips record label, and soon after this turned professional to back US R&B artists playing UK club dates; performers like Patti Labelle & The Blue Belles, The Drifters, Doris Troy and Billy Stewart.

ELTON AND BERNIE POSE FOR THEIR EARLIEST PUBLICITY PHOTOGRAPH TOGETHER, 1968

They were once lined up for a Wilson Pickett tour but Pickett's guitarist was not impressed with them and Pickett pulled out of the deal. It was shortly after this that they were signed up to tour with Major Lance, who later recommended the band to other R&B artists in the States. A recording session for their first single followed, and they recorded 'Come Back Baby' at the Philips Studios in London which was released on the Fontana label in July 1965.

Towards the end of 1966, Long John Baldry adopted Bluesology as his backing band, and expanded the group into a nine-piece, adding American guitarist Caleb Quaye, Elton Dean on saxophone plus Peter Gavin, Mark Charig and Neil Hubbard. Now known as 'The John Baldry Show', they moved on to the cabaret circuit. "It's the graveyard of musicians. I'd rather be dead than playing cabaret," said Elton. Bluesology released two further singles, one for Philips and another for Polydor, but neither troubled the chart compilers.

Thoroughly disillusioned by the summer of 1967, Elton auditioned for Liberty Records who were establishing an independent London office, and advertising for artists and writers at Regent Studios in Denmark Street. Elton sang two Jim Reeves songs, 'I Love You Because' and 'He'll Have To Go'. "I went for the appointment," remembers Elton. "I said I can't write lyrics and I can't sing really well, but I think I can write songs." Too nervous to perform any of his own compositions he failed, but was offered some lyrics sent in to Liberty by a would-be poet from Lincolnshire called Bernie Taupin. They began to correspond but did not meet until Elton had composed music for at least twenty of Bernie's songs.

Taupin, born on 22 May 1950, started writing scraps of poetry from an early age. He adopted a gypsy image with long hair, a single earring and tattered clothes and had spent two years travelling around England doing casual work. Like Elton, he'd come across the Liberty ad in *New Musical Express* although it was his mother who encouraged him to reply. On 7 November that same year, Elton and Bernie were signed to Dick James music publishing as staff writers, and so began the creative song writing partnership between Elton and Bernie...

1964-68

As a member of Bluesology, Elton pays his dues playing whenever and wherever the group get booked. As well as playing shows in their own right, they also become the backing band for visiting American R&B singers, including Billy Stewart, The Ink Spots, Patti Labelle and The Blue Bells, Major Lance, The Drifters and Doris Troy. To their eternal shame and disappointment, they are rejected by Wilson Pickett.

Elton: "Sometimes we did four gigs in one day, with someone like Billy Stewart. We did the US Serviceman's Club at Douglas House, Lancaster Gate, at around four in the afternoon, then we did the Ritz and the Plaza Ballroom in Birmingham and then we finished off by playing the Cue Club in Paddington at round six in the morning. If playing four gigs wasn't bad enough, we had to load up, unload and set up our own equipment at each gig."

One of the highlights for Reg during this period was a performance at the Cavern Club in Liverpool and, also following in the footsteps of The Beatles, gigs in Hamburg. Recalling the Cavern date, Elton recalls that the gig was marred by the toilets overflowing and threatening to damage their equipment.

ABOVE: BLUESOLOGY, WITH ELTON ON FAR RIGHT
LEFT: THE ORIGINAL ADVERTISEMENT FROM *NME* WHICH BROUGHT ELTON AND BERNIE TOGETHER

1966

DECEMBER

11 December

Bluesology are one of the support bands on the only London appearance of Little Richard at the Saville Theatre in Shaftesbury Avenue. The Bluesology line-up consists of Stuart Brown (vocals), Reg Dwight (keyboards), Freddie Creasey (bass), David Murphey (sax), Chris Bateson (trumpet) and Paul Gale (drums). Other support bands are The Quotations and The Alan Price Set.

1967

Bluesology become the regular backing band for blues singer Long John Baldry who in November tops the UK charts with an MOR ballad called 'Let The Heartaches Begin'. Baldry thereafter moves on to the UK cabaret circuit and Elton becomes very disheartened with the way his career is progressing.

Elton: "We started playing big ballrooms. The high spot of our act was when Baldry used to sing his hit ('Let The Heartaches Begin') to a backing tape that we had to mime to. As Baldry's style changed towards the soft ballady stuff, we moved into cabaret and it was really beginning to bring me down. We were the night club entertainment to help the food go down nicely. I began looking through the papers to try and find a job. I didn't care what it was, working in a record shop...anything..."

1968

MARCH
1 March
Elton débuts with the single 'I've Been Loving You' backed with 'Here's To The Next Time' on Philips. The song was written by Elton only, although the lyricist credit was given to Bernie Taupin.

APRIL
Elton starts recording demonstration versions of newly-written songs for Dick James Music and other music publishing companies, including many Roger Cook-Roger Greenaway compositions.

MAY
7 May
Elton plays his last Bluesology gig in Scotland. On the way home he adopts the name 'Elton John', taking the 'Elton' part from saxophonist Elton Dean and the 'John' part from Long John Baldry.

Elton: "(Reg Dwight) was hopeless. It sounded like a library assistant."

JUNE
7 June
Elton announces to close friends that his wedding to Linda Woodrow will take place at Uxbridge Registry Office at 9.45am, followed by a reception at 30a Frome Court on June 22.

16 June
Elton cancels his wedding plans.

DECEMBER
Elton records 'Lady Samantha' and 'All Across The Heavens' at the Dick James Studio in London. The two tracks will be released as Elton's second and final single on Philips on 17 January, and although it fails to chart, it does pick up significant UK radio airplay.

ELTON JOHN PICTURED HERE IN ONE OF HIS FIRST PUBLICITY SHOTS

1969

At various times during the year Elton plays sessions for 'soundalike' albums released by Music For Pleasure and Marble Arch Records. Like all the other performers on these sessions, he is uncredited.

JANUARY
Elton auditions as lead singer with Robert Fripp's new group King Crimson, but is turned down.

7 January
Elton writes 'Empty Sky' and 'Flowers Will Never Die'.

FEBRUARY
Caleb Quaye assembles a studio band for Elton that includes Nigel Olsson who had been drummer for Plastic Penny, The Spencer Davis Group and Uriah Heep, and Dee Murray, a bass guitarist who has also worked with The Spencer Davis Group. These two musicians would become Elton's closest musical collaborators after Bernie Taupin.

Elton plays on 'The Dick Barton Theme' backed with 'Breakdown Blues', released as a Bread And Beer Band single on the Decca label.

8 February
Lulu performs Elton and Bernie's 'I Can't Go On Living Without You' on her BBC TV show. It is one of the British entries for the Eurovision Song Contest.

APRIL
Elton goes into the Dick James Studios in London to record 'Just Like Strange Rain'.

10 & 11 April
Elton records 'It's Me That You Need' at Olympic Studios in Barnes.

MAY
16 May
'It's Me That You Need' backed with 'Just Like Strange Rain' is released as Elton's new single.

JUNE
Elton contributes 'From Denver To LA' to the soundtrack of the film *The Games*. The track is released on a single in the US in 1970.

Elton: "Actually, 'From Denver To LA' was withdrawn, so if you've got a copy it's worth a small fortune. It was a 25 quid session I did at Olympic Studios and I just sang the song, and it was for the Michael Winner movie The Games. And that's it. When the film was released EJ had just become successful in the States and so they thought Ahh ha! and rushed it out, but we quickly put an injunction on it and stopped it."

Elton does session work on cover version recordings for albums of soundalike tracks of current British hit singles.

3 June
Elton releases his first album 'Empty Sky'.

Elton: "Making the 'Empty Sky' album still holds the nicest memories for me, because it was the first I suppose. We used to walk back from the sessions at about four in the morning and stay at the Salvation Army headquarters in Oxford Street.

Steve Brown's dad used to run the place, and he used to live above it. "I used to sleep on the sofa. It's difficult to explain the amazement we felt as the album began to take shape, but I remember when we finished work on the title track... it just floored me. I thought it was the best thing I'd ever heard in my life."

25 June
Elton plays piano on The Hollies' studio session for 'He Ain't Heavy, He's My Brother' at Abbey Road Studios, London.

AUGUST
31 August
Elton sees Bob Dylan and The Band at the Isle Of Wight Pop Festival.

SEPTEMBER
21 September
Elton sees The Who at Croydon Fairfield Hall.

OCTOBER
27 October
Elton writes 'Your Song'.

1970

JANUARY
Elton goes into Trident Studios in Soho to start work on tracks for his second album. He records 'Border Song', 'Bad Side Of The Moon', 'Rock And Roll Madonna', 'Grey Seal', 'Your Song', and 'Into The Old Man's Shoes'.

16 January
The *NME* reports that the critics are unanimous in predicting Elton will be one of the most exciting discoveries of 1970.

MARCH
Elton goes into Trident Studios in London to start recording 'Tumbleweed Connection'.

20 March
'Border Song' backed with 'Bad Side Of The Moon' is released as Elton's new single. Although it receives substantial UK airplay, it fails to reach the UK chart.

APRIL
Dates: The Roundhouse Pop Proms (21).

Elton appears on *Top Of The Pops* performing 'Border Song'.

10 April
The 'Elton John' album is released to great reviews. Produced by Gus Dudgeon, it features the first Elton John Band comprising Elton on vocals and keyboards, Caleb Quaye on guitar, Dee Murray on bass and Nigel Olsson on drums. It reaches number 11 on the UK chart and, in October, number 4 on the US chart.

18 April
In the *Melody Maker* Richard Williams asks 'Is this the year of Elton John?'

Elton: *"I'd really like to do a couple of gigs a week, because that's how you sell yourself to people.* **Top Of The Pops** *doesn't really give anybody an idea of what you can do - in fact it gives them a totally wrong impression...*

"Bernie always writes the words of a song first and then gives them to me and I write the tune. It always works perfectly and I think we gain from doing it that way. I can't write lyrics and I know what Bernie wants, so it always comes out right. We don't write a lot - generally it comes in spasms when we feel like it...

"Bluesology would never let me sing, so I only really started when we were doing the first demos, and my voice improved - I hope - as I did more and more."

21 April
This is the début of Elton John with Dee Murray and Nigel Olsson. Headlining act is T.Rex.

25 April
Melody Maker reviews the 'Elton John' album, calling it "a truly great record".

MAY
Dates: Roundhouse, Chalk Farm (7).

9 May
Elton goes into Abbey Road Studios in St John's Wood to play piano for The Hollies on 'I Can't Tell The Bottom From The Top', and guests with the group on 'Perfect Lady' for inclusion on their album 'Confessions Of The Mind'.

JUNE
Dates: Marquee, Wardour Street, London (5), Lyceum, London (supporting Santana) (17).

6 June
NME reviews the 'Elton John' album, referring mainly to the accompanying press release and offering very little critical opinion.

ELTON WITH NIGEL OLSSON ON DRUMS, DEE MURRAY ON BASS AND DAVEY JOHNSTONE ON GUITAR

19 June
'Rock And Roll Madonna' backed with 'Grey Seal' is released as Elton's new single. It fails to chart. Accompanying the single is a DJM press release in which Elton is extolled by various writers: "Time to hail a new genius in the commercial folk world" - Don Short, *Daily Mirror*.

"As singer/songwriter he is emerging as one of the most fascinating new talents around" - Anne Nightingale, *Daily Sketch*.

"He is probably Britain's first real answer to Neil Young and Van Morrison." - Robert Partridge, *Record Mirror*.

"John is a brilliant composer (in partnership with Bernie Taupin) and a fine singer." - Richard Williams, *Melody Maker*.

"Elton John shares the distinction of creating music which strikes that rare balance between brilliance and honest originality." - Mark Williams, *International Times*.

JULY
Dates: Country Club, London (3).

Elton's first radio appearance on *Sounds Of The Seventies*.

AUGUST
Dates: Krumlin Festival, near Halifax (15), US tour (through to September). Troubadour, Los Angeles, USA (25).

Elton signs to Uni Records in the US, and releases 'Border Song' as his first single. It reaches 92 on the Billboard chart.

15 August
Although not billed as such, Elton is the star of the show at this small festival in Yorkshire. Despite atrocious weather, his enthusiasm - and the fact that he passes bottles of brandy into the audience - warms the crowd. He gets a rave review in *Melody Maker* from Chris Charlesworth for his efforts.

25 August
Elton's first live appearance in USA, opening the 20th anniversary celebrations for Doug Weston's Troubadour Club in LA, is an astounding success. This is followed by 17-date tour of the USA that includes dates at the Fillmore West in San Francisco where promoter Bill Graham re-books Elton.

SEPTEMBER
26 September
Melody Maker reports that Elton is storming the States on his current tour. In an interview with Richard Williams, Elton talks about his band with the line -up of Nigel Olsson and Dee Murray.

Elton *"It's a real band now, and the boys have helped me a lot. It's so tight now, but in a year's time it'll be unbelievable. America did our confidence a lot of good and I don't ever have to tell them what to do because we all know what we're doing. There are some songs with very broken rhythms, but they just play them without having it explained to them."*

OCTOBER
Dates: Royal Albert Hall, London (2), USA tour (through to December 18).

Elton records 'Friends' and 'Honey Roll' at Trident Studios in London.

30 October
Elton releases 'Tumbleweed Connection' which reaches number 6 on the UK chart, and number 5 on the US charts.

Elton: *"I like 'Empty Sky' because of its naïvety. 'Elton John' because it was panic stations, 'Tumbleweed Connection' because aside from the bits I don't like, there are bits I do like. It was funky and in retrospect, it was quite a bold step to take after the 'Elton John' album."*

NOVEMBER
Dates: Santa Monica Civic Auditorium (15), Fillmore East, New York, USA (20 & 21), San Francisco Fillmore West, San Bernadino Swing Auditorium.

17 November
Elton records the album '17-11-70' as a live radio broadcast in front of a small audience at A&R Studios, New York. The decision to release it is influenced by the existence of bootleg LPs circulating in the US.

20 November
Elton starts two nights of concerts at the Fillmore East in New York with Leon Russell. Bob Dylan visits Elton backstage.

21 November
Bob Dylan returns to visit Elton's concert at the Fillmore East in New York with his wife Sarah, Paul Simon and ex-Papa John Phillips. Dylan's apparent enthusiasm for Elton inspires *Melody Maker's* memorable banner headline, 'DYLAN DIGS ELTON!'.

28 November
Melody Maker reports that Elton's first headlining British tour will take place from 2 January to 28 March, and that Elton will return to America from 1 April to 15 May, and will spend the following three months in Europe, but it's a massive US tour from September through to November which ensures his dollar millionaire status.

DECEMBER
Dates: Anaheim Convention Center, California, USA (4), Roundhouse, London (20).

4 December
The set for this concert features a selection of the following: 'Your Song', 'This Is My Life', 'Can I Put You On', 'Honky Tonk Woman', 'Burn Down The Mission', 'Get Back', 'My Baby Left Me'.

20 December
This is a charity show, headlined by The Who. During The Who's set Pete Townshend dedicates the evening's performance of 'Tommy' to Elton and predicts a promising future for him.

1971

JANUARY

Dates: Mother's, Birmingham (2), Pavilion, Hemel Hempstead (3), Country Club, Hampstead (8), Guildford Civic Hall (10), Winter Gardens, Cleethorpes (11), City Hall, Hull (13), Southampton University (15), Loughborough University (16), Paris TV (17,18), Liverpool Philharmonic (27), Lancaster University (29), Big Apple, Brighton (30), Fox, Croydon (31).

In the *NME* 1970 poll, Elton is voted fourteenth world male singer and world musical personality. In the British section, he is ninth vocal personality, top new disc singer, and eighth male singer.

2 January
Elton starts his first UK tour at Birmingham.

14 January
'Your Song' is featured on *Top Of The Pops*.

15 January
The Watford Observer reports how Elton has been acclaimed by music critics and disc jockeys as a superstar and the most exciting musical discovery since The Beatles.

23 January
Melody Maker reports from the first Midem Music Festival Gala concerts that Eric Burdon blasted Elton away from the stand in Cannes, France. Elton, representing Britain, and Eric, representing America, were booked to appear in the gala concerts, but the timing of the shows allowed only 14 minutes for each act. Burdon and his American band War roar away for an hour and ten minutes, playing continuously and refusing to leave the stage despite pleas from the organisers. A furious Elton refuses to follow Eric and storms out of the theatre.

Elton releases his new single, 'Your Song' backed with 'Into The Old Man's Shoes', which reaches number 7 in the UK chart and number 8 in the US.

30 January

Elton fails to appear at the Big Apple Club in Brighton where hundreds of fans have bought tickets to see him. It is alleged that the promoter of the concert knew that Elton was pulling out over a fortnight ago, but the Big Apple Club failed to make any announcements until after the doors were opened.

FEBRUARY

Dates: Cooks Ferry Inn, Edmonton (1), Lanchester Arts Festival (5), Leeds University (6), Bumpers, London (9), Stirling University (12), Strathclyde University, Glasgow (13), Dunfermline Kinema (14), Newcastle-upon-Tyne City Hall (20), Imperial College, London (24), Brunel University, Uxbridge (26), Bradford University (27).

Cancelled Tour Dates: Top Rank, Cardiff (8), Electric Garden, Glasgow (15), Tiffany's, Edinburgh (16), Caird Hall, Dundee (17), Music Hall, Aberdeen (18), Osprey Room, Aviemore (19). These dates were cancelled on medical advice that Elton should curtail his commitments due to the pressure of sustained work during the past few months. Elton is awarded an RIAA gold disc in the US for sales worth one million dollars for the 'Elton John' album.

6 February

Melody Maker starts 'The Elton John Story' - the fascinating story of the rise of a new superstar.

27 February

Elton records 'Goodbye' at Trident Studios, London.

MARCH

Dates: Royal Festival Hall, London (3), Leicester University (6), Kingston Polytechnic (13), Colston Hall, Bristol (14), University College, London (20), Croydon, Fairfield Hall (28).

Cancelled Tour Dates: Chez Club, Leytonstone (5), Leeds Polytechnic (26), Roundhouse, Dagenham (27). These dates were cancelled on medical advice due to the pressure of sustained work during the past few months, and

ELTON JOHN

Original Soundtrack Recording
A Film by LEWIS GILBERT

"friends"

A Paramount Picture

that Elton should curtail his commitments.

Elton is awarded a RIAA gold disc in the US for sales worth one million dollars for the 'Tumbleweed Connection' album.

3 March

For the Royal Festival Hall concert, Elton is backed by a full orchestra conducted by Paul Buckmaster. The programme is selected from the following: 'Talking Old Soldiers', 'Levon', 'Where To Now St Peter', 'Country Comfort', 'Honky Tonk Women', 'Amoreena', 'Can I Put You On' (with Nigel Olsson & Dee Murray), 'Take Me To The Pilot', 'I Need You To Turn To', 'First Episode At Hienton', 'Border Song', 'Your Song', 'The King Must Die', 'Sixty Years On', 'The Greatest Discovery', 'Love Song', 'My Father's Gun', 'Burn Down The Mission', 'Come Down In Time', 'Friends', 'Goodbye' (with orchestra).

5 March

The 'Friends' album is released, peaking at number 36 in the US Top 40 album chart.

11 March

Elton guests on BBC TV's *Andy Williams Show*.

APRIL

Dates: Providence, RI (2), Boston, Mass (3), Philadelphia, Pa (4), New York, NY (9/10), Baltimore, Md (11), Chicago, Ill (14/15), Detroit, Mi (16), Columbus, Ohio (17), Cincinnati, Ohio (18), Portland, Wa (21), Vancouver, Canada (23), Seattle, Wa (24).

Elton releases his first live album titled '17-11-70'. It reaches number 20 on the UK chart and number 11 on the US chart.

1 April

Elton arrives in the USA for concert tour.

3 April

A British television documentary about Elton is featured in the LWT series *Aquarius*. It shows Elton at home, in rehearsal and in concert.

9 April

Elton is awarded a RIAA gold disc in the US for sales worth one

million dollars for the 'Friends' album. The award is presented to Elton backstage at the Fillmore East, New York City.

23 April

'Friends' backed with 'Honey Roll' is released as Elton's new single. It makes Number 34 in the US, but fails to reach the UK chart.

MAY

Dates: Honolulu, Ha (1), San Francisco, Ca (9), Sacramento, Ca (11), Fresno, Ca (12), Anaheim, Ca (14), Denver, Co (16), Boulder, Co (17), Oklahoma, Ok (19), Houston, Tx (20), San Antonio, Tx (21), Dallas, Tx (22/23), Fort Worth, Tx (24), New Orleans, Lo (26), Tampa Curtis Hixon Hall, Fl (28), Miami, Fl (29), Jacksonville, Fl (30).

8 May

Melody Maker reports from Los Angeles that..."Elton seems to be having a problem in the central part of the USA. His concerts have not been selling out and in the words of one observer, he's dead in New York. And everyone knows New York is the centre of popular opinion".

15 May

Melody Maker reports from Los Angeles that Elton's concert at the Anaheim Convention Center on 14 May is completely sold out. The supporting acts are Redeye and Mark Almond.

29 May

The *NME* concludes its three-part 'Chat In' series with Elton, who talks about Englishmen liking American things, doing Educational TV pop shows, being on the *Andy Williams TV Show*, the British TV scene and greedy artists. Parts 1 and 2 appeared in the 15 and 22 May issues respectively.

JUNE

Dates: St Louis (4), Memphis (5), Louisville (6), Atlanta (8), New York (10/11), Cleveland (12), Providence (13).

10 June
Elton is pictured on the front cover of *Rolling Stone* magazine.

Elton: *"Bernie and I do seem to attract weirdos. I don't know why, because we're not really weird ourselves. People give me pineapples, and some girl gave me her knickers. Yeah, in Scotland, some girl took off her knickers and threw them on stage - along with a bowler hat, can you get that one together?"*

20 June
Elton returns from America, having been there since the beginning of April. He returns there again on 25 August for another long tour, until the end of October.

23 June
Elton is guest on BBC TV's *It's Cliff Richard* show.

JULY
Dates: Crystal Palace, London (31).

31 July
For this special concert at Crystal Palace, Elton is supported by Yes, Rory Gallagher, Fairport Convention, Hookfoot and Tir Na Nog. The set features a selection from the following: 'Skyline Pigeon', 'Rock Me When He's Gone', 'I Need You To Turn To', 'Tiny Dancer', 'Love Song', 'Razor Face', 'Indian Sunset', 'Whole Lotta Shakin'.
Melody Maker announces that Elton's British tour is scheduled to take place in November and December.

AUGUST
Dates: Syracuse, NY (26), Wildwood, NJ (27), Asbury Park, NJ (28), Milwaukee, Wi (30).

7, 9, 11 & 14 August
Trident Studios, London. Recording tracks for 'Madman Across The Water'.

21 August
Melody Maker reports that Elton leaves for the USA on 25 August, playing coast to coast until 18 September. Following a short rest he goes to Japan for Tokyo concerts, then to Australia to play major cities.

18

SEPTEMBER

Dates: Saratoga Springs, NY (2), Syracuse, NY (3), Rochester, NY (4), Los Angeles, Ca (6-12), Las Vegas, Ne (15), Reno, Ne (16).

18 September

In the *Melody Maker* readers' 1971 poll, Elton is fourth best male singer in the British section and 'Your Song' is sixth best single. In the International section, he is third best pianist/organist and sixth best composer.

OCTOBER

Dates: Venue, Washington DC, USA (16).

16 October

Elton gives a concert for the Joseph P Kennedy Foundation for the Mentally Retarded Children in Washington DC.

28 October

Rolling Stone reports that... "Elton was the latest of a series of freaks to be refused admission to Disneyland. Despite his short hair and the company of his Mum and Dad, Elton was turned out because of numerous patches on his jeans. But John convinced the guards that the Disneyland concessions sold patches, and was let back in."

NOVEMBER

Dates: Coventry Theatre (21), Free Trade Hall, Manchester (22), De Montfort Hall, Leicester (24), Winter Gardens, Bournemouth (26), ABC Theatre, Plymouth (27), Colston Hall, Bristol (28).

2 November

Elton returns to Britain from a mini world tour which took in concerts in America, Australia and Japan.

5 November

Elton releases his new album 'Madman Across The Water'. It reaches number 41 on the UK charts and number 8 on the US.

Elton: *"I was on tour in New York and Long John Baldry rang me up from London and told me that Warner Brothers wanted him to do an album ('It Ain't Easy'), and he had this idea for Rod (Stewart) to produce one side, and for me to do the other side. I hadn't ever done any producing and the idea gave me the horrors, but nevertheless I said yes because I like John."*

13 November

Elton talks to Bob Randall of the *NME* on the perils of over-exposure.

Elton: *"I'm determined to cut down on work. I'll be doing less touring and putting more time aside for recording and writing. I've got the British tour to do, but next year I must have time to think and write. When I think about it, it's a wonder I've survived the last few months."*

21 November

Elton's first British tour for a year begins. The support act is Texas duo England Dan & John Ford Coley.

DECEMBER

Dates: Town Hall, Birmingham (3), Dome, Brighton (4), Fairfield Hall, Croydon (5), City Hall, Newcastle-upon-Tyne (10), ABC Theatre, Stockton-on-Tees (11), Town Hall, Leeds (16), City Hall, Sheffield (24).

7 December

Elton is interviewed on BBC TV's *Old Grey Whistle Test* and performs 'Tiny Dancer' and 'All The Nasties'.

8 December
Elton records a 47 minute slot on *Sounds For Saturday* for transmission on 29 April, 1972.

25 December
Billboard's year-end analysis of the album charts shows Elton as sixth most successful artist of the year, while *Cashbox* year-end analysis of the album charts shows Elton as joint top male vocalist with James Taylor.

27 December
Elton plays piano with T. Rex on live studio performance of 'Get It On' on *Top Of The Pops.*

1972

JANUARY
Elton records 'Rocket Man' and other tracks for his next studio album at Strawberry Studios, Château D'Hierouville, in France.

1 January
A new single is released in America titled 'Levon'. It reaches number 24 on the *Billboard* chart.

7 January
Reginald Kenneth Dwight formally changes his name by deed poll to Elton Hercules John.

22 January
In the *NME* 1971 readers' poll, Elton is voted sixteenth world male singer and twentieth world musical personality. In the British section, he is thirteenth male singer and fifteenth vocal personality.

FEBRUARY
Dates: University of Lancaster (19), Exeter University (23), Watford Town Hall (24) Waltham Forest Technical College (26).

Ex-Magna Carta guitarist Davey Johnstone joins Elton's band. Elton is awarded a RIAA gold

disc in the US for sales worth one million dollars for the 'Madman Across The Water' album.

19 February
Support act for this gig is Brinsley Schwarz. This is the début of Elton's new band comprising Nigel Olsson, Dee Murray and Davey Johnstone.

23 & 24 February
Support act for these gigs is Linda Lewis.

26 February
Support act for this gig is Sunshine.

MARCH
Dates: Frankfurt (12 & 20).

11 March
Elton talks to NME's Julie Webb.

Elton *"I've never regarded pop music as an art form - I think it is just entertainment and I think that is why pop groups are coming back because people are fed-up with moodies and they'd rather go out and have a good time."*

APRIL
Dates: Waco, Tx (26), Houston, Tx (28), Austin, Tx (30).

22 April
Elton releases a new single titled 'Rocket Man' backed with 'Holiday Inn' and 'Goodbye'. It reaches number 2 in the UK and number 6 in the US.

ELTON AND BERNIE WITH GOLD RECORD FOR THE 'ELTON JOHN' ALBUM

MAY

Dates: Columbia, Mo (2), South Bend, Ind (3), East Lansing, Mi (4), Dayton, Ohio (5), Columbia, Ohio (6), Oxford, Ohio (7), Urbana, Ill (10)

John Reid leaves his job at EMI Records to become Elton's personal manager.

19 May

Elton releases a new studio album titled 'Honky Château'. It reaches number 2 in the UK and number 1 in the US.

Elton: *"For a start there's no orchestra and there are rock'n'roll tracks which we've never done before on albums. I don't want to say it's the best thing I've ever done because that's what I said and felt about 'Madman' but people didn't agree. It's just that with this album no-one can turn around and say, 'Oh, it's Elton John with his bloody 100 piece orchestra again'. There's one number on the album called 'I Think I'm Going To Kill Myself' which I think is going to have tap dancing on it. A sort of vaudeville number. I guarantee the numbers on the album will get many covers because the songs are light pop."*

JUNE

Elton records 'Crocodile Rock', 'Elderberry Wine', 'Daniel' and a new version of 'Skyline Pigeon' at the Strawberry Studios in France.

18 June

Elton is interviewed by Michael Beatty on Radio One.

30 June

Elton is interviewed for *The Beatles' Story* on Radio One.

JULY

18 July

Elton is interviewed by Michael Beatty on Radio One about the 'Honky Château' album.

24 July

Elton is awarded a RIAA gold disc in the US for sales worth one million dollars for the 'Honky Château' album.

31 July

Elton is again interviewed for '*The Beatles' Story*' on Radio One.

AUGUST

Dates: Guildhall, Portsmouth (26), Shaw Theatre, London (27), City Hall, Newcastle-upon-Tyne (31).

26 August

For the first date of the tour Linda Lewis is the support act, and the musicians backing Elton are again Dee Murray on bass, Nigel Olsson on drums and Davey Johnstone on guitar. These are the only UK concerts as Elton is set to tour America from the middle of September.

SEPTEMBER

Dates: Free Trade Hall, Manchester (1), Fairfield Hall, Croydon (3), Greens Playhouse, Glasgow (8), New Theatre, Oxford (10), Ithica, NY (26), Boston, Mass (27/28), New Haven, Ct (29), Philadelphia, Pa (30),

9 September

A new single is released. 'Honky Cat' backed with 'It's Me That You Need' and 'Lady Samantha' peaks at number 31 in the UK and number 8 in the US.

16 September

Elton tells *Disc* about the formation of the Rocket Record Company.

"What we are offering is undivided love and devotion, a fucking good royalty for the artist and a company that works its bollocks off."

23 September

NME's Julie Webb talks to Elton at his home in Surrey for an article 'Down At Elton's Funky Château'.

Elton: *"I'm sure singles do help an album. And I'm also sure you can afford to have two hit singles off an album. Singles now are getting much better, a lot more people are putting out maxi singles which is a good state to be in. But I won't necessarily be tied to releasing singles off albums - if I suddenly come out with a monster song I'd probably go in the studios and work it out. Yet at the same time I've now started to put out albums with singles on them."*

OCTOBER

Dates: Rochester, NY (1), Montreal (2), Toronto (5), Detroit, Mi (6), Buffalo, NY (7), Long Island, NY (9), Normal, Ill (11), Wichita (12), Ames, Iowa (14), Denver, Co (15), Honolulu (18), Seattle, Wash (20), Berkeley, Ca (21), Anaheim, Ca (22), Los Angeles, Ca (23), Berkeley, Ca (25), Tucson, Az (26), San Diego, Ca (27), London Palladium (30).

Elton makes guest appearance in Marc Bolan's movie *Born To Boogie*, performing 'Children Of The Revolution' with Marc Bolan and Ringo Starr.

27 October

'Crocodile Rock' backed with 'Elderberry Wine' is released as Elton's new single. Both are tracks from the forthcoming album 'Don't Shoot Me, I'm Only The Piano Player'. The single reaches number 5 in the UK and number 1 in the US.

30 October

Elton makes his first appearance on the Royal Variety Show at the London Palladium, performing 'I Think I'm Gonna Kill Myself' with Legs Larry Smith doing a tap dance.

NOVEMBER

Dates: Stillwater, Ok (1), Tulsa, Ok (2), Oklahoma City, Ok (3), Kansas City, Mo (4), Dallas, Tx (5), College Station, Tx (8), San Antonio, Tx (9), Baton Rouge, Lo (10), Memphis, Tenn (11), Nashville, Tenn (12), Scope Auditorium, Norfolk, Va (13), Tuscaloosa, Fla (14), Atlanta, Ga (15), Charlotte, NC (16), Charleston, NC (17), Hampton Roads, Va (18), New York City, NY (19/20), Baltimore, Md (21), Harrisburg, Pa (22), Jacksonville, Fla (24), Miami, Fla (25), St Petersburg, Fla (26).

11 November

Julie Webb catches up with a tired Elton for the *NME* and reports how he has had to reshuffle several gigs on his American tour and cancel out completely in Phoenix in order to appear on the Royal Variety show.

NIGEL OLSSON, LEGS LARRY SMITH, ELTON, DAVEY JOHNSTONE AND DEE MURRAY

13 November

Davey Johnstone does not appear at this concert due to illness. The set features a selection of the following: 'Tiny Dancer', 'Daniel', 'Susie', 'Your Song', 'Levon', 'Can I Put You On', 'Goodbye Yellow Brick Road', 'Mona Lisas And Mad Hatters', 'Honky Cat'.

DECEMBER

Dates: Scope Auditorium, Norfolk (13).

Elton, Marc Bolan and Ringo Starr perform 'Children Of The Revolution' in an excerpt from the film *Born To Boogie* shown on BBC TV's *Old Grey Whistle Test*.

21 December

The Daily Express reports that Elton has bought a 2ft high antique musical box from Fortnum & Mason as a Christmas gift for a friend at a cost of £1,000.

30 December

Elton talks to Tony Norman who writes a short autobiography titled 'Elton - The Embarrassed Genius' for *NME*.

ELTON WITH MARC BOLAN AND RINGO STARR AT THE PREMIERE OF BOLAN'S 'BORN TO BOOGIE' FILM

1973

JANUARY

6 January

The famed *Melody Maker* team of writer Chris Welch and photographer Barrie Wentzell visit Elton's home in Surrey for an article titled 'Inside Elton's Honky Château'. Elton talks about his upcoming 'Don't Shoot Me I'm Only The Piano Player' album and the pressures of fame.

Elton *"We made the album last June, and it seemed like it would never come out. But I wanted a long gap and we only had one LP out last year. I didn't want the situation where every few months there was an Elton John album out.*
"I really believe fame can make you into a withdrawn case. Look at George Harrison, Dylan, Presley, Lennon and Cassidy - they rarely go out.

I love success. If I don't enjoy it what would be the point? But I know a lot of stars who don't get enjoyment out of it and are really miserable. I love going out - I'm not going to become a hermit for anyone. Mind you, when you get plagued by autograph hunters, and you are right in the middle of a meal - that's a bit of an aggravation."

10 January

A second single from 'Don't Shoot Me, I'm Only The Piano Player', 'Daniel' backed with 'Skyline Pigeon', reaches number 4 in the UK and number 2 in the US. The single is featured on *Top Of The Pops* on 25 January. It later transpires that Elton and his management and recording company were at loggerheads over the release of 'Daniel'.

Elton: *"Dick James said he didn't want another single released to detract from sales of the new album, so I've more or less forced him to put it out. He has disowned it, so I am having to pay for all the advertising. But he says he will pay for the adverts if the single makes the Top Ten. Isn't that nice?"*

13 January

Elton sees Eric Clapton's comeback concert at the Rainbow Theatre in London.

20 January

Ken Evans visits New York at the invitation of Elton to see his performance at Carnegie Hall, and interviews Elton about his live performances past and future for an *NME* supplement.

Elton: *"I've never really done a major British tour so I really would like to do one of about three and a half weeks and do ballrooms and places like that. There's definitely going to be a big tour, either in February or March. We do neglect England but it is just finding the places and the time to play. I find touring rather boring, not the gigs, but driving to Bolton isn't quite as glamorous as driving to Santiago. But we really have got to get our finger out to do it. We did a short tour of England just before we came on this one and it really was amazing. There were great crowds and we owe it to them to go out there and do it again."*

YEARS BEFORE HIS AFFILIATION WITH PEPSI COLA, ELTON SIPS DOUBLE DIAMOND AND CHATS WITH DJ JOHN PEEL BETWEEN NUMBERS

26 January
Elton releases a new studio album titled 'Don't Shoot Me, I'm Only The Piano Player'. It reaches number 1 in both the UK and US charts.

FEBRUARY
Dates: Greens Playhouse, Glasgow (25), Birmingham Town Hall (28).

3 February
In *Melody Maker*, a full page ad announces the formation of the Rocket Record Company by Elton, Bernie Taupin, Gus Dudgeon, John Reid and Steve Brown.

17 February
The *NME* reports on the 'Fighting Side of Elton John' - the star who hates those men in the music industry with big fat cigars, and how he's starting his own record label to prove it.

20 February
Bob Harris interviews Elton on the *Old Grey Whistle Test.*

Elton: *"I know I haven't the best image for rock and roll and that probably gets in the way of my music sometimes. But most of my clothes are just for a laugh."*

25 February
Elton's UK tour begins with usual musicians Dee Murray on bass, Davey Johnstone on guitar and Nigel Olsson on drums.

MARCH
Dates: De Montfort Hall, Leicester (1), Empire, Liverpool (2,3), Guildhall, Preston (6), City Hall, Newcastle-upon-Tyne (7), City Hall, Sheffield (9), Leeds University (10), Colston Hall, Bristol (15), Dome, Brighton (16), Winter Gardens, Bournemouth (17), Guildhall, Southampton (18), Sundown, Mile End Road (22), Sundown, Edmonton (23), Sundown, Brixton (24), Coventry Theatre, Coventry (25), Hard Rock, Manchester (26, 27).

Elton sets up Rocket Records in Wardour Street, London. The label will initially provide an outlet for other artists.

23 March
Rod Stewart appears on stage to present Elton with a bouquet of flowers for his birthday on the 25th.

31 March
Melody Maker reports that Elton is now a teen idol who attracted screamers to his two sell-out concerts at London's Sundown Theatre last week.

APRIL
7 April
Melody Maker's Chris Charlesworth reports how Elton is mobbed for the first time on his recent British tour, and how at Newcastle, Elton's promoter broke his ankle fighting to keep fans at bay..

Elton: "We don't carry around a heavy mob, and if the stage is low we have to watch out for them. It took us an hour to get out of a building in Glasgow, and we've had to use decoys because we were trapped. There were times when I thought the fans would rip us apart. I'd rather they lined up in a line for two hours and I signed autographs for them, but they wouldn't do that".

MAY
Elton goes to the Strawberry Studios in France to record 'Saturday Night's Alright For Fighting', 'Jack Rabbit', 'Whenever You're Ready', 'Goodbye Yellow Brick Road', 'Screw You', 'Candle In The Wind', 'Bennie And The Jets' and 'Harmony'.

6 May
Elton is interviewed for *The Rolling Stones' Story* on Radio One.

JUNE
29 June
Elton releases his new single 'Saturday Night's Alright For Fighting' backed with 'Jack Rabbit' and 'Whenever You're Ready'. It reaches number 7 on the UK charts and number 12 on the US.

Elton: "I'm getting a bit fed-up with singer-song-writer records. They drive me mad. I was labelled a singer-song-writer and did four LP's in that syndrome. But I've always fought against the Elton John syndrome. People take it too seriously. I'd like us to be a band. On the first albums we used a lot of session men, but we could never do it that way now, planning it down to the last flute."

JULY
28 July
CJOM FM Ontario begins a two-part series titled *The Elton John Story*. Part two is broadcast on 29 July.

AUGUST
8 August
Elton is interviewed for *The Beatles Story* on Radio One.

15 August
Elton begins his US tour, which will run through to 21 October. The set for this tour features a selection of the following: 'Honky Cat', 'Goodbye Yellow Brick Road', 'Rocket Man', 'All The Young Girls Love Alice', 'Daniel', 'Madman Across The Water', 'Teacher I Need You', 'Crocodile Rock'.

22 August
Elton is interviewed for *The Story Of Pop* on Radio One.

30 August
Radio One begins a two-part profile of Elton and Bernie Taupin titled *The Poet And The Pub Pianist*. It is presented by Brian Matthew who is featured in conversation with Elton. Part two is broadcast on September 15.

SEPTEMBER
Dates: Hollywood Bowl, Los Angeles, USA (7), Madison Square Garden, New York (23).

7 September
'Goodbye Yellow Brick Road' backed with 'Screw You' is released as Elton's new single. The A-side is the title track from the forthcoming album. It reaches number 6 on the UK charts and number 2 on the US charts. In the US the B-side had to be retitled and became 'Young Man's Blues'.

31

15 September

Melody Maker's Chris Charles-worth reports on Elton's Hollywood Bowl concert, calling it Elton's finest hour. Elton is introduced on stage by porn star Linda Lovelace, and is preceded by lookalikes of numerous celebrities, including The Beatles, Frankenstein, Marilyn Monroe, The Pope, Graucho Marx and even The Queen of England.

OCTOBER

5 October

Elton releases his new album 'Goodbye Yellow Brick Road'. It reaches number 1 on both the UK and US charts.

NOVEMBER

Trident Studios, London. Recording 'Step Into Christmas' and 'Ho! Ho! Ho! Who'd Be A Turkey At Christmas'.

24 November

Elton talks to Chris Welch for a *Melody Maker* interview.

Elton: *"I'm so glad I grew up in the early pop era. If I was growing up now, it wouldn't be the same. Perhaps I'm getting old but there's not so much magic in Donny Osmond as there was, say, in Ricky Nelson. Everything is so disposable, especially in the States, not so much here. In the old days, pop records weren't made because they sounded chic. It was done out of complete naïvety. Everything is done now for a motive."*

26 November

'Step Into Christmas' backed with 'Ho! Ho! Ho!' is released as Elton's new single. It reaches number 24 on the UK charts.

DECEMBER

Dates: Odeon, Hammersmith, London (20-24).

4 December

Elton is the subject of Bryan Forbes' second documentary for British Television. *Elton John & Bernie Taupin Say Goodbye To Norma Jean And Other Things* is shown on the ITV network.

8 December

The *Melody Maker* reviews Elton's performance at Belle Vue, Manchester, calling it "sensational".

22 December

Radio One FM live broadcast of this concert at Odeon Hammersmith. The set features a selection of the following: 'Funeral For A Friend', 'Love Lies Bleeding', 'Candle In The Wind', 'A Cat Named Hercules', 'Rocket Man', 'Bennie And The Jets', 'Daniel', 'This Song Has No Title', 'Honky Cat', 'Goodbye Yellow Brick Road', 'The Ballad Of Danny Bailey 1909-34', 'Elderberry Wine', 'Rudolph The Red Nosed Reindeer', 'I've Seen That Movie Too', 'All The Young Girls Love Alice', 'Crocodile Rock', 'Your Song', 'Saturday Night's Alright For Fighting'. The band line-up comprises Dee Murray, Nigel Olsson, Davey Johnstone, Ray Cooper and Clive Banks.

23 December

Demand for tickets for the Odeon Hammersmith Christmas concerts is so great that Elton is obliged to add a matinée performance.

1974

JANUARY
Elton records 'Don't Let The Sun Go Down On Me', 'The Bitch Is Back' and 'Cold Highway' at the Caribou Ranch, Colorado.

30 January
Elton is interviewed for *The Story Of Pop* on Radio One.

FEBRUARY
4 February
'Bennie And The Jets' is released as Elton's new single in America and it crashes into the US chart at number 1. In the UK, the track is released as the B-side to 'Candle In The Wind'.

28 February
Some Auckland roads are jammed for several hours as 34,000 people travel to Western Springs Stadium to see Elton in concert.

MARCH
Dates: Randwick Racetrack, Australia (14).

6 March
The Daily Telegraph reports that Elton's manager John Reid is to serve a month in jail in New Zealand for assaulting a journalist and a woman writer on the eve of Elton's concert in Auckland.

14 March
The set for this concert features a selection of the following: 'Funeral For A Friend', 'Love Lies Bleeding', 'Candle In The Wind', 'Goodbye Yellow Brick Road', 'Bennie And The Jets', 'Honky Cat', 'Your Song'.

23 March
The *Melody Maker* reports that Elton has postponed next month's mammoth British concert tour because of fatigue.
The tour, originally scheduled to begin at Paignton's Festival Hall on 28 April, would have finished at London's Empire Pool, Wembley. The European dates of the tour were due to start the following week but these too have been cancelled.

APRIL
More recording sessions at the Caribou Ranch, Colorado, USA where Elton tapes 'Sick City'. Further sessions at the Rampart Studios, London provide the 'Pinball Wizard' track for the movie of Pete Townshend's rock opera 'Tommy'.

10 April
Elton attends Eric Clapton's comeback party at the China Garden Restaurant in Soho, London.

20 April
An editorial portrait of Elton as a football tycoon appears in *NME*.

MAY
Dates: Vicarage Road, Watford (5), Royal Festival Hall, London (18), Empire Pool, Wembley (27).

5 May
Rod Stewart joins Elton on stage at Watford Football Club for a benefit concert in aid of the club.

16 May
'Don't Let The Sun Go Down On Me' backed with 'Sick City' is released as Elton's new single. It reaches number 16 on the UK charts and number 2 on the US charts.

18 May
This concert is taped for later album release.

JUNE
Elton at the Caribou Ranch, Colorado, to record 'Someone Saved My Life Tonight' and 'House Of Cards'.

19 June
MCA Records announce the signing of Elton to a long term recording agreement, and take out full page ads in the *New York Times* and *Los Angeles Times*.

22 June
Billboard reports that Elton re-signed with MCA Records for what label president Mike Maitland calls "the best deal anybody ever got".

ELTON, APPROPRIATELY DRESSED IN A HORNET'S OUTFIT. WITH ROD STEWART ON STAGE AT WATFORD FOOTBALL GROUND

NIGEL OLSSON, RAY COOPER, ELTON, DAVEY JOHNSTONE AND DEE MURRAY

THE ENTIRE CREW OF 35 FOR ELTON'S 1974 US TOUR

Elton is rumoured to be receiving $8 million in advances by the end of the deal, plus new high percentages on his existing catalogue product. Maitland and vice president Lou Cook first talked with Elton in Chicago, hammered out the contract with him during five days in London and eventually signed in New York.

28 June
Elton releases his new album 'Caribou'. It reaches number 1 on both the UK and US charts.

Elton: "It was recorded under the most excruciating of circumstances. We had eight days to do fourteen numbers. We did the backing tracks in two and a half days. It drove us crazy because there was a huge Japanese tour, then Australia and New Zealand, that could not be put off. And it was the first time we had recorded in America, and we just couldn't get adjusted to the monitoring system which was very flat. I never thought we'd get an album out of it."

29 June
Elton talks to *Melody Maker's* Allan Jones about his new album 'Caribou'.

Elton: "I thought it would get slagged off, because it seemed the time for something of mine to get slagged. I think the British press might have decided it's time to knock me again, so I'm just sitting back and taking it."

JULY
Caribou Ranch, Colorado, USA. Recording 'Lucy In The Sky With Diamonds' (with John Lennon on guitar), 'One Day At A Time' and 'Philadelphia Freedom'.

9 July
Elton performs 'Ticking' and 'Grimsby' on BBC TV's *Old Grey Whistle Test*.

13 July
Elton signs the $8 million contract with MCA.

AUGUST
Tickets for Elton's October concerts in Los Angeles sell out in minutes, causing a further show to be added.

30 August
Elton releases a new single titled 'The Bitch Is Back', from the album 'Caribou'. The B-side, 'Cold Highway' is exclusive to the single. It reaches number 15 in the UK and number 4 in the US.

SEPTEMBER
Dates: Baton Rouge

16 September
Elton tells David Wigg in his *Daily Express* interview that he refuses to let his massive fortune get him down.

Elton: "A lot of stars shut them-selves away and become recluses. But I really enjoy life at the top."

OCTOBER
Dates: The Forum, Los Angeles, USA (5), Seattle Or (13), Portland (15).

'Whatever Gets You Through The Night' is released as the new single by Elton and John Lennon. It reaches number 36 on the UK chart and number 1 in the US.

5 October
The set for this concert features a selection from the following: 'Grimsby', 'Rocket Man', 'Take Me To The Pilot', 'Bennie And The Jets', 'Grey Seal', 'Daniel', 'You're So Static', 'Lucy In The Sky With Diamonds', 'Don't Let The Sun Go Down On Me', 'Honky Cat'. The Muscle Shoals Horns join Elton's regular band line-up.

19 October
Melody Maker chronicles Elton's giant US tour with a special two-page spread titled 'On Tour With Elton'.

NOVEMBER
Dates: Madison Square Garden, New York, USA (28, 29).

8 November
A compilation album of 'Elton's Greatest Hits' is released. It reaches number 1 in both the UK and US.

9 November
In the Melody Maker American special report from Vancouver, Ritchie Yorke describes Elton's North American tour as "the most successful ever by a British artist."

28 November
John Lennon joins Elton on stage at Madison Square Garden, New York and duets on 'Whatever Gets You Through The Night', 'Lucy In The Sky With Diamonds' and 'I Saw Her Standing There'.
Apparently Elton and Lennon had a bet: if Lennon's 'Whatever Gets You Through The Night' reached number one in the *Billboard* Hot 100, then he (Lennon) would perform with Elton on stage at the Garden.

Lennon was reported to have been terrified before going on stage and the tumultuous reception he received almost reduced him and Elton to tears. It turns out to be Lennon's final appearance on any stage before a live audience.

Elton: "We did 'I Saw Her Standing There' which was great and I was so glad we did that. Originally I said, 'Let's do two numbers, but you'll have to do another.

Why not do 'Imagine'?' He said, 'Oh no, boring. I've done it before. Let's do a rock and roll song. So I thought of 'I Saw Her Standing There' which was the first track on the first Beatles album. And he never sang it. It was McCartney who sang it. John was so knocked out because he'd never actually sung the lead before.

For us it was very emotional and one rock paper crucified us. But it was just an emotional night and nobody could believe it. I knew John would be petrified about doing it, but he really enjoyed it. I was more scared than he was, hoping things would go right for him. But the reaction when he walked on stage...

I wish he could have done more numbers because the reaction was so great. But he wanted to go upstairs and be sick. He told me he used to throw up before he went on stage. He came to Boston to see us before we did New York, and I've never seen anyone so nervous in my life. He was so worried for us."

ELTON AND JOHN LENNON ON STAGE AT MADISON SQUARE GARDEN, NOVEMBER 28, 1974

DECEMBER
Dates: Odeon, Hammersmith, London (24).

21 December
Elton tells *Melody Maker's* Chris Welch:

"I only play for pleasure when I write. I never sit down and play, but if I do I always try and sing other people's songs. I like doing sessions. I used to do a lot of sessions at one time, and I miss doing them. People won't ring me any more because they think I'm too busy. I did Rod's and Lennon's things. They were not really sessions, just friends asking me down. And I did a Neil Sedaka and Ringo Starr."

23 December
The Daily Telegraph reports on Elton's Hammersmith appearances saying that no amount of spangled gimmickry, clowning or noise can hide his great talent as a musician and a performer of good songs, and that his precision is unfailing and never becomes mechanical.

24 December
Rod Stewart and Gary Glitter join Elton on stage at his Hammersmith Odeon concert in London. The concert is simultaneously broadcast live by BBC 2's *Old Grey Whistle Test* and Radio One. Transmitted footage includes 'Bennie And The Jets', 'Lucy In The Sky With Diamonds', 'I Saw Her Standing There', 'Don't Let The Sun Go Down On Me', 'Honky Cat', ' Saturday Night's Alright For Fighting', 'Crocodile Rock', 'The Bitch Is Back', 'Your Song', and 'White Christmas'. Songs unseen by television viewers include 'Grimsby', 'Rocket Man', 'Goodbye Yellow Brick Road', 'Daniel' and 'Grey Seal'.

ELTON, NEIL SEDAKA AND BERNIE

1975

JANUARY

3 January
Reports in the press suggest that Elton is planning to play the star role in a rock opera version of *Hamlet*, with words and music by himself and his partner Bernie Taupin. The stories go on to say that Ken Russell may direct, and that David Bowie would be taking part as a singing, dancing Ophelia, but "utter nonsense" was the retort from Elton's manager John Reid.

13 January
Elton's album 'Empty Sky' is re-released in the US and reaches number 6 on the *Billboard* chart.

FEBRUARY

22 February
Roy Carr and Charles Shaar Murray examine 'The Life and Times of Elton' in the *NME*. Part 2 appears in the March 1 issue and Part 3 on March 8.

28 February
'Philadelphia Freedom' is released as Elton's new single. The B-side, 'I Saw Her Standing There', was recorded live at Madison Square Garden with John Lennon. It reaches number 12 in the UK and number 1 in the US.

MARCH

15 March
Elton refuses to appear on British TV. He cancels an appearance on *Top Of The Pops* , and claims his decision will extend to all TV shows in the UK. The move stems from a Musicians' Union rule stating that artists must re-record songs in order to perform them on TV.

28 March
Elton presents his own show on Radio One - *Don't Shoot Me, I'm Only The Disc Jockey*.

APRIL
Ken Russell's film version of The Who's 'Tommy' is released. It features Elton and The Who performing 'Pinball Wizard'.

19 April
Elton fires band members Dee Murray and Nigel Olsson on the eve of the release of the autobiographical album 'Captain Fantastic And The Brown Dirt Cowboy'. Conflicting reports in *NME* suggest that the split from the band is less than amicable.

Elton: "I've never fired anybody in my life. Both members took it very hard. I did them both by phone. Nigel was in LA... he actually took it worse than Dee to start with.

But since then I've seen Nigel a lot and he's actually closer to me now than he's ever been. Even though underneath it all, he's still deeply hurt. Dee, however, is not talking to me. We've only had the one phone call. I phoned up and asked him out to dinner and he wouldn't go. He's a little hurt and I can understand that...

"It's an impossible sort of situation saying to someone after five years that they're out and that's it. But give it a little time and things will work out."

MAY

23 May

Elton releases a new album titled 'Captain Fantastic And The Brown Dirt Cowboy'. It reaches number 2 on the UK charts and number 1 in the US.

JUNE

Dates: Wembley Stadium (21), Oakland Coliseum, USA (29).

1 June

Elton rehearses with new band in Amsterdam for the Wembley Stadium gig later this month. The line-up is Davey Johnstone and Caleb Quaye on guitars, Kenny Passerelli on bass, James Newton-Howard on keyboards, Ray Cooper on percussion, Roger Pope on drums, plus three back-up singers.

Elton: "It's fulfilling one of my lifelong ambitions. I've always wanted to be part of a good driving rock and roll band. The old band never used to drive - we used to rattle on. Whenever we played anything live, it was always twice the tempo of the recording and it was a bit off-putting to me. I want to chug rather than race. It's good to be racy sometimes, but now I want to rock and roll in a laid-back manner, and with this band I've got the chance of doing it. This band chugs."

21 June

Elton headlines at Wembley Stadium with The Beach Boys, The Eagles, Jo Walsh, and Rufus and Stackridge in support, and Johnnie Walker compères. Elton unwisely chooses to perform all the songs from the new 'Captain Fantastic' album, thus inflicting on the audience a massive dose of music with which they are completely unfamiliar. According to press reports, many of them walk out.

28 June

Elton releases 'Someone Saved My Life Tonight' backed with 'House Of Cards' as the new single. The A-side is a partly autobiographical account of Elton's recent suicide attempt. It reaches number 22 on the UK charts and number 4 in the US.

29 June

At an Oakland Coliseum concert by The Doobie Brothers and The Eagles, Elton jams on stage with both bands on 'Listen To The Music' and Chuck Berry's 'Carol'.

JULY

Elton at the Caribou Ranch, Colorado to record 'Island Girl', 'Sugar On The Floor', 'Grow Some Funk Of Your Own' and 'I Feel Like A Bullet'.

6 July

The Sunday Times reports that Jimmy Connors, the American tennis champion, is involved in discussions with an American company to make a pop record, and that he has the backing of Frank Sinatra and Elton.

AUGUST

Dates: The Troubadour, Los Angeles, USA (25, 26), San Diego Sports Arena, California, USA (29).

11 August

Elton is named as outstanding rock personality of the year in the first rock music awards in Santa Monica.

25 & 26 August

Elton plays two benefit shows at LA's Troubadour for UCLA's Jules Stein Eye Institute, raising over $150,000.

29 August

The set for this concert features a selection from the following: 'Meal Ticket', 'Island Girl', 'Philadelphia Freedom', 'Better Off Dead', 'Harmony', 'Captain Fantastic & The Brown Dirt Cowboy', 'Someone Saved My Life Tonight', 'Don't Let The Sun Go Down On Me'. The band line-up is

comprised of Davey Johnstone, Ray Cooper, James Newton-Howard, Caleb Quaye, Roger Pope and Kenny Passerelli.

SEPTEMBER
17 September
The Daily Telegraph reports that Elton is buying a house for a figure close to £400,000. The mansion, which stands in 37 acres, dates from the reign of Queen Anne and contains six principal bedroom suites. There is a huge garden, swimming pool with changing pavilion and a coach house block with garaging, stabling, staff cottage and groom's flat.

19 September
'Island Girl' backed with 'Sugar On The Floor' is released as the new single. It reaches number 14 on the UK chart and number 1 in the US.

OCTOBER
Dates: Portland Memorial Coliseum (14), Dodger Stadium, Los Angeles, USA (25).

4 October
Elton releases a new album titled 'Rock Of The Westies'. It reaches number 5 on the UK chart and number 1 on the US chart.

NOVEMBER
Dates: Dodger Stadium, Los Angeles, USA (26).

8 November
Elton becomes godfather to John and Yoko Lennon's son, Sean.

SEAN LENNON

15 November
The *NME* reports that Elton and John Reid have forked out £50,000 to fly out their relations, friends, employees and a handful of journalists to celebrate Elton's weekend Dodger Stadium gigs on the West Of The Rockies US tour. The set for this tour features a selection of the following: 'Your Song', 'I Need You To Turn To', 'Dan Dare', 'Levon', 'Country Comfort', 'Rocket Man', 'Hercules', 'Empty Skies', 'Someone Saved My Life Tonight', 'Lucy In The Sky With Diamonds', 'I Saw Her Standing There', 'Pinball Wizard' and 'Saturday Night's Alright For Fighting'.

21 November
Elton receives a star on Hollywood's Walk of Fame as Los Angeles declares 'Elton John Day'.

26 November
Elton concludes his West Of The Rockies US tour at the Dodger Stadium in Los Angeles dressed in a sequined Dodgers uniform, and becomes the first artist to play at the venue since The Beatles in 1966.

DECEMBER
10 December
The *Daily Mirror* reports that Elton is locked in a legal battle with American tax authorities over his vast earnings. Box office receipts from every concert he has given in the States since 1973 - estimated at more than £3 million have been frozen, although the precise details of why are unknown.

ELTON JOHN

1976

JANUARY

9 January

'Grow Some Funk Of Your Own' backed with 'I Feel Like A Bullet' is released as Elton's new single. It fails to chart in the UK, but reach-es number 14 in the US.

FEBRUARY

14 February

Melody Maker announces details of Elton's forthcoming Spring tour, which is his first since the Wembley Stadium gig in June 1975. It is estimated 160,000 will see this tour.

MARCH

7 March

Elton is immortalised in wax at Madame Tussaud's in London. He is the first rock star since The Beatles to be so honoured.

12 March

'Pinball Wizard' backed with 'Harmony' is released as Elton's new single. It reaches number 7 on the UK chart.

22 March

Elton records 'Don't Go Breaking My Heart' and 'Snow Queen' as duets with Kiki Dee. Also 'Sorry Seems To Be The Hardest Word', 'Shoulder Holster', 'Crazy Water', 'Chameleon' and 'Bite Your Lip' at Eastern Studios in Toronto.

APRIL

Dates: Leeds, Grand Theatre (29/30).

30 April

Elton releases his new album 'Here And There', a live album recorded in London and New York. It reaches number 6 on the UK chart and number 4 in the US.

The *Daily Telegraph* magazine charts the success of Elton in an article titled 'Captain Fantastic He Is' as Elton starts out on a tour of Britain.

MAY

Dates: Manchester, Belle Vue (1), Preston Guildhall (2), Liverpool Empire (3,4), Leicester, De Montfort Hall (5), Stoke On

Trent, Victoria Hall (6), Wolverhampton, Civic Hall (7), Croydon, Fairfield Hall (9), London, Earls Court (11,12), Watford, Bailey's Club (14), Birmingham, Odeon (16,17), Sheffield, City Hall (18), Newcastle, City Hall (20), Edinburgh, Usher Hall (21), Dundee, Caird Hall (22), Glasgow, Apollo (24,25), Coventry New Theatre (27,28), Southampton, Gaumont (29), Taunton, Odeon (30), Bristol, Hippodrome (31).

2 May

The Sunday Times reports that five thousand fans were evacuated from the King's Hall, Belle Vue, Manchester after a bomb scare during Elton's concert. They were allowed back half an hour later.

5 May

Radio One begins a seven-part series titled *The Elton John Story*. It is written and presented by Paul Gambaccini. Parts two, three, four and five, are broadcast on May 11, 18, 25, and June 9 respectively, while parts six and seven are held over until 1977 on February 24 and March 30.

8 May

The *Melody Maker* reports on Elton's concert at the Grand Theatre in Leeds.

"This was Elton being Elton, with no trimmings. There were no stage props or gimmicks in sight, not a whiff of dry ice, and not even a back projection screen."

11 & 12 May

Proceeds from these two concerts at Earls Court, London, benefit the Sports Aid Foundation.

14 May
The Guardian reports that Elton last night staged one of the most ambitious events ever held to raise money for sport in Britain when he gave the second of his two concerts in London. The two evenings played to full houses of 12,000 at Earls Court and will provide about £40,000 for the Sports Aid Foundation, the body launched last October to raise money for outstanding British sportsmen.

Elton: "No one realises how much sport means to people in this business."

JUNE
Dates: Cardiff, Capitol (3, 4).

21 June
'Don't Go Breaking My Heart' backed with 'Snow Queen' is released as the new single by Elton and Kiki Dee. It reaches number 1 in the UK and US. Despite his massive global success this is actually Elton's first UK number one hit single.

Elton performs 'Don't Go Breaking My Heart' with Miss Piggy on TV's The Muppet Show.

Elton: "Everyone knows I'm desperately in love with Miss Piggy. I'm doing a TV show in America, but she will not be my guest because I gather she is signed up by The Muppets. So I haven't mentioned it to her. Kermit explained to me that she can be impulsive and pigheaded - and if I invited her on the show and she broke her contract all hell would break loose."

27 June
At the evening show during an Elvis Presley tour in Largo, Maryland, Elton meets Elvis backstage during the intermission.

JULY
Dates: Foxborough, Mass (4).

1 July
The Daily Mirror reports that Elton's house in Virginia Water, Surrey, has failed to attract a buyer at the quoted figure of £125,000, and he has now reduced the price to around £80,000.

13 July
The Daily Mirror reports that Elton is being sued for £30,000 after a row at a hotel swimming pool. The claim, which seeks damages for slander, was filed by Frank Grassie. He said that Elton had him thrown out of a hotel in Atlanta, Georgia.

22 July
Elton and Kiki Dee perform 'Don't Go Breaking My Heart' on Top Of The Pops.

AUGUST
Dates: Madison Square Garden, New York, USA (10-13, 15-17).

10 August
Elton begins a seven-date series of sell-out concerts at New York's Madison Square Garden, breaking the house record set a year earlier by The Rolling Stones.

14 August
Melody Maker's Chris Charlesworth, covering Elton's current US tour, reports that Elton's gig at the Edinburgh Playhouse on September 17 will be his last concert anywhere in the world for at least 18 months. He has decided to concentrate on production for Rocket Records and his Directorship of Watford FC.

Elton: "I've done it for six years and I'm fed up with it. I'm not so much fed up with playing, but I'm fed up with having no base and constantly roaming around. I'm not retiring, just laying off for a while."

ELTON WITH KIKI DEE

His popularity in America is another reason for quitting.

Elton *"It's got so big for me over there it's getting stupid. I cannot switch off, and it's beginning to be a little bit of a bore. I can't live my life in a shell like Elvis Presley. I want to do something positive with my life, and getting involved with Watford Soccer Club is my way of doing it."*

SEPTEMBER
Dates: Edinburgh Playhouse (17).

9 September
Elton releases 'Bennie And The Jets' backed with 'Rock And Roll Madonna' as his new single. It reaches number 37 on the UK charts and number 1 in the US.

17 September
Edinburgh Playhouse.
Elton makes a guest appearance at Kiki Dee concert, performing 'Don't Go Breaking My Heart'.

Elton: *"I'm definitely not retiring but I want to put my energies else-where for a while. Y'know, I feel really strange at this particular point in time. I always do things by instinct and I just know it's time to cool it, I mean, who wants to be a 45 year old entertainer in Las Vegas like Elvis?"*

OCTOBER
7 October
Elton is pictured on the front of *Rolling Stone* magazine with the headline 'Elton's Frank Talk - The Lonely Love Life Of A Superstar'. During the course of a long

interview with Cliff Jahr printed inside, Elton talks on the record about his bisexuality for the first time. It will prove to be a watershed in his life and career.

Elton: *"There's nothing wrong with going to bed with somebody of your own sex. I think everybody's bisexual to a certain degree. I don't think it's just me. It's not a bad thing to be. I think people should be free with sex... they should draw the line at goats."*

10 October
'Sorry Seems To Be The Hardest Word' backed with 'Shoulder Holster' is released as Elton's new single. It reaches number 11 on the UK chart and number 6 in the US.

20 October
Launch party at 17 Savile Row in London for the release of the 'Blue Moves' album and Elton's retirement from live work. Estimated cost is £2,180.

22 October
Elton releases his new album 'Blue Moves'. It reaches number 3 in the UK and US.

DECEMBER
11 December
Elton is interviewed on BBC News about Watford FC.

25 December
Elton is special guest on *The Morecambe & Wise Christmas Show* and performs 'Shine On Through' from the 'Single Man' album.
Elton performs 'Don't Go Breaking My Heart' with Kiki Dee on *Top Of The Pops Christmas Show*.

1977

JANUARY

25 January
Elton remixes 'Can't Buy You Love'. This was originally recorded in Seattle, Washington with Thom Bell. Elton is not happy with the original mix.

27 January
Elton talks to David Wigg of *The Daily Express* on sex, drugs, taxes, fans, punk rock, love and marriage.

Elton: "I've had five or six great years but I have to say goodbye to that era, I have to start from the word go again. Thinking this way kicks me up the rear...
"I would rather have a wife and children because I adore children, that's one of the things I would really like to do...

"Sure, I'm earning more than a doctor or a nurse, but then I'm paying more to help bail out this country. I think people tend to forget that a lot of the time".

FEBRUARY
4 February
Elton releases a new single titled 'Crazy Water' backed with 'Chameleon'. It reaches Number 27 on the UK chart.

MARCH
Recording 'The Goaldigger Song' charity record, featuring Elton, Jimmy Hill, Brian Moore and Eric Morecambe. Only 500 copies are pressed for 'Goaldiggers', a football charity.

APRIL
10 April
The Sunday Express reports that Elton and his manager John Reid are to open an eating establishment in London's Covent Garden and intend to call it Friends.

15 April
Elton talks about his career on *Rock On* on Radio One.

MAY
Dates: Rainbow Theatre, London (2-7)

2 May
Elton, accompanied by Ray Cooper on assorted percussion instruments, opens a six night run at the Rainbow Theatre in London. The opening night, a gala performance in aid of The Queen's Silver Jubilee Appeal is attended by Princess Alexandra and Angus Ogilvy.

4 May
The Daily Telegraph reports that Elton has apologised to Princess Alexandra for repeating details of a private conversation. The Princess had asked him at a backstage party following the charity concert on 2 May if he used cocaine. Elton later repeated the remark to reporters.

Elton: "I very much hope I have not embarrassed the Princess. I thought it was very amusing and that is why I repeated it. Of course, I do not take cocaine. It was only meant as a light-hearted comment."

8 May
The Sunday Times reports how John Reid built a pop empire. When he took over the management of Elton, they set themselves a gruelling work schedule. In a 12 month period in 1971-72, Elton recorded two albums, made two concert tours of America, and one each of Britain, Europe, Scandinavia, Japan, Australia and New Zealand. All were accompanied by as much attention grabbing ballyhoo as Reid could dream up.

28 May
Elton takes part in the Royal Windsor Big Top Show in the presence of Her Majesty The Queen and Prince Philip. The show is recorded in Billy Smart's circus tent at Home Park, Windsor, for screening on BBC-TV on 29 May.

JUNE
Dates: Rainbow Theatre, London (11).

3 June
'Bite Your Lip' backed with 'Chicago' is released as Elton's new single. It reaches number 28 in both the UK and US.

Radio One broadcasts Elton's concert at the Rainbow Theatre, London.

11 June
Elton achieves a lifetime ambition when he becomes Chairman of Watford Football Club.

SEPTEMBER
13 September
A second compilation album of 'Elton's Greatest Hits' is released. It reaches Number 6 on the UK chart and Number 21 in the US.

OCTOBER
1 October
Elton becomes the first rock artist to be honoured in Madison Square Garden's Hall Of Fame, in New York.

Elton records 'Are You Ready For Love Parts I and II' at the Kay Smith Studio, Seattle, USA & Sigma Sound Studios, Philadelphia, with US producer Thom Bell.

NOVEMBER
Dates: Empire Pool, Wembley (3).

3 November
Elton announces that he is to retire to an audience of 12,000 from the stage of the Empire Pool, Wembley, during a special charity performance in aid of the Royal Variety Club of Great Britain and the 'Goaldiggers' who raise money for football pitches and facilities for under-privileged children.

Elton: *"Thank you very much. I really enjoyed tonight. But this is going to be the last show. There's a lot more to me than playing on the road."*

The support band at this show is China, who also happen to be Elton's own band. They consist of Davey Johnstone and Joe Partridge on guitars, James Newton-Howard on keyboards, Cooker Lo Presti on bass and Dennis Conway on drums.

DECEMBER
25 December
Elton guests on *The Morecambe & Wise Christmas Show* on BBC TV.

ELTON AND JOHN PEEL BACKSTAGE AT THE 1977 READING FESTIVAL

ELTON WITH PERCUSSIONIST RAY COOPER

1978

JANUARY

Elton starts recording at the Mill Studio, Cookham, Berks. These sessions last through to September.

10 January

Elton talks to the *American People* magazine about the time he tried to commit suicide. "It was a very Woody Allen type suicide. I turned on the gas and left all the windows open". The attempt to kill himself was the result of his first and only serious love affair. He was 21 and had made all the arrangements to marry a 6ft 2in blonde girl. The experience inspired him to write 'Someone Saved My Life Tonight'.

MARCH

10 March

Elton records 'Ego', 'Flintstone Boy', 'Part-Time Love' and 'I Cry At Night' at the Mill Studio, Cookham, Berks.

21 March

'Ego' backed with 'Flintstone Boy' is released as Elton's new single. It reaches number 34 on both the UK and US chart.

APRIL

16 April

Elton is profiled in *The Sunday Times* magazine.

Elton: "Most people have completely the wrong idea of me. They think I'm going to go on doing the same things in glittering clothes, going to Las Vegas till I'm 55. I turned down one offer of a million dollars to do a week in Vegas. I didn't even think about it. No, I'm looked upon as one of the artists in this country who has the least credibility and I think I have the most credibility."

19 April

The Sun reports that Elton has launched an astonishing attack on Britain's pop charts. He said the British Market Research Bureau chart - the one the BBC uses - was "highly inaccurate".

Elton: "Everybody in the business knows it's ridiculous. But far too few people have had the courage to say so. Until something is done about it, I have decided to withdraw my record company's advertising from any publication printing the BMRB chart."

26 April

The Daily Mail reports that within days of Elton branding the BBC Top Twenty chart as "inaccurate", his record company has been threatening members of its staff with the sack unless his latest song 'Ego' gets on *Top Of The Pops*. And in a late night call from Australia, Elton's manager John Reid tells two senior employees that they can consider themselves relieved of their jobs if a promotion film made by Elton does not appear on the programme, but Reid explains, "It was all done in a fit of anger. I was furious because they hadn't explored the possibilities of getting the record played over the credits at the end and told them

they hadn't done their jobs properly. I have apologised for screaming so loudly and I have said we shall talk about it when I return to London on Sunday."

AUGUST

18 August

Elton records 'Song For Guy'.

OCTOBER

4 October

Elton releases a new single titled 'Part Time Love' backed with 'I Cry At Night'. It reaches number 15 on the UK chart and number 22 in the US.

16 October

Elton releases his new album titled 'A Single Man'. It reaches number 8 on the UK chart and number 15 in the US.

NOVEMBER

7 November

Elton collapses at his home and is rushed by ambulance to the Harley Street Clinic's coronary care unit in London. According to press reports, Elton suffered an attack of chest pains at his home in Windsor. Friends said he had been recovering from a month of intensive promotion for the new album 'A Single Man'. A spokesman for the Harley Street Clinic said Elton was conscious when he was admitted "as an investigative case" and also denied that he had suffered a heart attack, but would not reveal the nature of his illness.

28 November

A new single is released in Britain titled 'Song For Guy' which is dedicated to Guy Burchett, a young messenger who worked for Elton's Rocket Record Company, and who died in a tragic road accident. The single, backed with 'Lovesick', reaches number 4 on the UK chart.

DECEMBER

7 December

Elton joins Eric Clapton on stage for 'Further On Up The Road' at the Civic Hall, Guildford.

WITH ERIC CLAPTON

1979

JANUARY

9 January
Elton takes part in a concert to start the International Year of the Child, and gives his services free, as do Olivia Newton-John, Rod Stewart, John Denver, Abba and The Bee Gees.

FEBRUARY
Dates: Stockholm, Concerthalls (5 & 6), Copenhagen, Tivoli (7 & 8), Hamburg, Musikhalle (10), Le Hague, Congresshalle (11), Rotterdam, Doelin (12), Amsterdam, Concertgebau (14), Mannheim, Mozarthalle (15), Munich, Deutsches Museum (16), Berlin, Kongresshalle (18), Cologne, Opera House (19), Paris, Champs Elysée (20-25), Antwerp, Queen Elizabeth Hall, London (26-27).

5 February
Elton's first live appearance since 'retiring' from live work. This tour, dubbed the Single Man Tour, features Elton accompanied solely by Ray Cooper on percussion.

MARCH
Dates: Düsseldorf, Philipshalle (1), Wiesbaden, Rhein Main Halle (2), Lausanne, Téâtre Di Bealiieu (3 & 4), Nice, Téâtre De Verdure (6 & 7), Madrid, The Real Madrid Pavilion (9-11), Glasgow Apollo (17 & 18), Edinburgh, Odeon (19), Newcastle City Hall (21 & 22), Preston, Guildhall (23), Belfast, Whitla Hall (26 & 27), Dublin, National Stadium (29 & 30).

6 March
Elton is named as top British singer by listeners of London's Capital Radio for the third year running.

APRIL
Dates: London, Drury Lane (2-7), Brighton, Dome (9 & 10), Southampton, Gaumont (11 & 12), Bristol, Hippodrome (14 & 15), Oxford Theatre (17), Coventry Theatre (18), Derby, Assembly Rooms (19), Birmingham, Hippodrome (21 & 22), Manchester, Apollo (24-26)

19 April
Elton announces details of his tour of the Soviet Union. He will give four concerts in Leningrad and four in Moscow between 21 and 30 May. The two-week tour will be filmed for British TV and one of the concerts will be broadcast live on BBC Radio.

30 April
Elton releases a new single titled 'Are You Ready For Love'. It reaches number 42 on the UK chart.

MAY
Dates: Great October Hall, Leningrad (21-24) Rossya Hall, Moscow (25-28).

20 May
Elton is nervous on the flight from London to Moscow. He is concerned about audience reaction during his four concerts in Leningrad and four more in Moscow.

21 May
The Daily Telegraph reports that Elton arrived in Moscow last night to take the Red Arrow train to Leningrad at the start of a ten-day concert tour. As he arrived it is announced that all seats for his first concert have been sold.

22 May
The Daily Mail reviews Elton's first concert in Leningrad claiming 'he won the acclamation of an audience that almost deafened itself in its own applause'.

28 May
Elton's concert at the Rossya Hall, Moscow is broadcast live on Radio One.

31 May
Elton arrives back in Britain after his successful eight-concert tour of the Soviet Union.

Elton: *"It was one of the most memorable and happy tours I've been on. The country is not dark, grey, grim or drab - it's beautiful and the people are very warm. Leningrad was a marvellous city, and the hospitality tremendous. The only negative experiences I had were two or three hangovers from vodka - marvellous stuff - and the Russian equivalent of the BBC doorman - little fat women with buns in their hair who stop you going where you want to go. This was the first time they had really experienced rock and roll at the level we gave them. We played 'Back In The USSR' every night without anyone objecting."*

JUNE
A new single is released in the US titled 'Mama Can't Buy You Love'. It reaches number 9 on the *Billboard* chart.

AUGUST
Recording sessions at Superbear Studios in Nice, Musicland in Munich, Sunset Sound in Los Angeles, and Rusk Sound Studios in Hollywood.

SEPTEMBER
Dates: Los Angeles, USA (26,27).

14 September
'Victim Of Love' backed with 'Strangers' is released as the new single. It fails to chart in the UK but reaches number 31 in the US.

26 September
The set for the opening night of this two-night concert features a selection of the following: 'I Heard It Through The Grapevine', 'I Feel Like A Bullet', 'Bennie And The Jets', 'Tonight', 'Better Off Dead', 'Idol', 'I Think I'm Gonna Kill Myself'.

27 September
Elton collapses on stage at Hollywood's Universal Amphitheater, suffering from exhaustion due to a bout of flu. After recovering and resting for ten minutes, he re-takes the stage for a three-hour show.

OCTOBER
Dates: Los Angeles (6), Chicago (11), Palladium, New York (18-20), Ann Arbor, Mi (29), Boston.

1 October
Elton's manager John Reid is arrested for allegedly attacking a hotel doorman with a walking stick. Reid lost his temper over a car parked outside the Fairmont Hotel in San Francisco.

13 October
Elton releases his new album 'Victim Of Love'. It reaches number 41 on the UK chart and number 35 in the US.

NOVEMBER
Dates: Tower Theater, Philadelphia (3), Modern Palladium, Sydney (27).

5 November
Elton talks frankly in an exclusive interview with The *Daily Mirror*.

DECEMBER
'Johnny B Goode' backed with 'Thunder In The Night' is released as Elton's new single. It fails to chart.

1980

JANUARY
18 January
The Daily Express reports that Elton's mother is moving away from her son's Windsor mansion. She has bought a house near Brighton, and will no longer be popping in every day to make sure Elton's smalls are laundered.

MARCH
17 March
Elton records 'Cartier Commercial' in Los Angeles.

28 March
Elton records 'Little Jeannie' in Los Angeles after the basic tracks have been recorded in August 1979 in Nice.

APRIL
11 April
Elton records 'Donner Pour Donner' with France Gall in Los Angeles. The song is composed by Bernie Taupin and Michael Berger.

MAY
1 May
Elton releases a new single 'Little Jeannie' backed with 'Conquer The Sun'. It reaches number 33 on the UK chart and number 3 in the US.

13 May
Elton releases a new album '21 At 33'. The title refers to Elton's 21st album in his 33rd year. It reaches number 12 on the UK chart and number 13 in the US.

JUNE
Dates: Detroit (9).

8 June
Elton records 'Fanfare' and 'Chloe' for the album 'The Fox'.

JULY
5 July
The *Daily Mirror* reports that Elton is suing for breach of contract over the country mansion he bought for £380,000 five years ago, claiming the estate is worth at least £50,000 less than he paid for it.

30 July
Elton is interviewed by Andy Peebles on Radio One.

AUGUST
5 August
'Sartorial Eloquence' backed with 'White Man Danger' and 'Cartier Commercial' is released as Elton's new single. It reaches number 44 in the UK and number 39 in the US. In the US the A-side is entitled 'Don't You Wanna Play This Game No More'.

7 August
The Daily Express reports that Elton was allowed to sit in the Speaker's chair after a lavish party at the House of Commons. The party was to launch the *Guinness Book of Hits of the Seventies*. Other guests included Gary Glitter, Freddie Mercury, and Bob Geldof.

SEPTEMBER
Dates: Rosemont Horizon, Chicago, Ill (5), Maple Leaf Gardens, Toronto (7&8), Civic Center, Providence, RI (11), Central Park, New York (13), Civic Centre, Baltimore, Md (16), Reynolds Coliseum, Raleigh, Va (20), Centennial Hall, Toledo, Ohio.

Elton co-writes 'Never Gonna Fall In Love Again' with Tom Robinson.

13 September
Elton's concert in New York's Central Park, for which he wears a yellow and blue Donald Duck outfit, attracts almost 500,000 fans. The concert is broadcast live and filmed for subsequent broadcast on British TV and for release as a commercial video in 1986.

21 September
Elton signs to Geffen Records in the US.

26 September
The Sun reports on Elton's spending sprees on priceless paintings, costly cars and glittering gems. In America, dollar bills are issued bearing his picture; Elton joins 40 other stars, including Sinatra, Elvis and Ronald Reagan, who receive the the same treatment.

OCTOBER
Dates: The Myriad, Oklahoma City, USA (9), Reunion Arena, Dallas, Texas, USA (16), Oakland Coliseum (24).

9 October
Judie Tzuke is the support act at this concert.

13 October
A new compilation album of Elton's best known hits is released. 'The Very Best Of Elton John' reaches Number 24 in the UK chart. A second compilation album of DJM label rarities is also released, but only in Britain. 'Lady Samantha' reaches number 56 on the UK chart.

14 October
Paul Gambaccini visits Elton in his home and discusses his many hits, his relationship with Bernie Taupin and the pressures of his career.

NOVEMBER
Dates: Anaheim Convention Centre, Ca (3), Forum, Los Angeles (6).

14 November
A new single is released titled 'Dear God' backed with 'Tactics'. It fails to chart.

DECEMBER
8 December
John Lennon is shot outside his apartment in New York. Elton, in Australia, arranges a special service at St Patrick's Cathedral in Melbourne, where he sings the 23rd Psalm and reads a lesson.

1981

MARCH
1 March
The Sunday Express reports that Prince Andrew has asked Elton to perform at his 21st birthday party. Elton responds saying he would jet the 7,000 miles back to England from Los Angeles where he is currently based, for just that one night.

13 March
Elton's live tracks with John Lennon as recorded at the Madison Square Garden concert are re-released as a tribute to Lennon. 'I Saw Her Standing There' coupled with 'Whatever Gets You Through The Night' and 'Lucy In The Sky With Diamonds'. It reaches number 40 on the UK chart.

APRIL
29 April
Radio One interviews Elton on buying the *Goon Show* scripts that were auctioned by Spike Milligan despite objections from other Goon members and the BBC.

MAY
8 May
Elton releases 'Nobody Wins' backed with 'Fools In Fashion' as his new single. It reaches number 42 in the UK and Number 21 in the US.

20 May
Elton releases a new album titled 'The Fox'. It reaches number 12 on the UK chart and number 21 on the US chart.

JULY
3 July
'Just Like Belgium' backed with 'Can't Get Over Losing You' is released as Elton's new single. It fails to chart.

1982

FEBRUARY
9 February
Elton records 'Blue Eyes' in Montserrat.

MARCH
Dates: Sydney Opera House (19).

Elton's first tour for two years opens in New Zealand.

12 March
'Blue Eyes' backed with 'Hey Papa Legba' is released as the new single. It reaches number 8 on the UK chart and number 12 on the US chart.

25 March
Elton receives gold disc award for 'Jump Up' album in New Zealand where it reaches number 1.

APRIL
Dates: Paris (17), Stockholm (30).

Elton records 'Empty Garden' in Montserrat.

9 April
Elton releases his new album 'Jump Up'. It reaches Number 13 on the UK chart and number 17 in the US.

MAY
Dates: Brussels (9), Lyons (25), Avignon (26).

28 May
Elton releases his new single titled 'Empty Garden' backed with 'Take Me Down To The Ocean'. The A-side is a tribute to John Lennon. It reaches number 51 on the UK chart and number 13 in the US.

JUNE
Dates: Irving Meadows, Ca (19), Hollywood Bowl, Los Angeles, Ca (26)

JULY
Dates: Starlight Theater, Kansas City, Ka (7), Poplar Creek, Chicago (11), Pipe Knob, Clarkstone (17), Performing Arts Center, Saratoga (25).

AUGUST
Dates: Boston Garden, Boston, Mass (3), Madison Square Garden, New York (5-7).

SEPTEMBER
Dates: Los Angeles (25).

'Princess' backed with 'The Retreat' is released as the new single. It fails to chart.

NOVEMBER
Dates: Newcastle-upon-Tyne, City Hall (2 & 3), Edinburgh, Playhouse (4 & 5), Dundee, Caird Hall (6), Glasgow, Apollo Theatre (7 & 8), Sheffield, City Hall (10 & 11), Liverpool, Empire Theatre (13 & 14), Blackpool, Opera House (15 & 16), Manchester, Apollo Theatre (17, 18 & 19), Birmingham, Odeon (21, 22 & 23), Cardiff, St David's Hall (25 & 26), Nottingham, Royal Concert Hall (27 & 28).

2 November
Elton starts his first major British concert tour for five years and is rejoined by his original band of Davey Johnstone, Dee Murray and Nigel Olsson.
  'All Quiet On The Western Front' backed with 'Where Have All The Good Times Gone?' is released as Elton's new single. It fails to chart.

12 November
A new compilation album is released. 'Love Songs' reaches Number 39 on the UK chart.

DECEMBER
Dates: Bournemouth, Winter Gardens (3 & 4), Southampton, Gaumont Theatre (5 & 6), Brighton Centre (7), Odeon, Hammersmith (9-24).

4 December
Elton is interviewed on BBC News about Watford FC opening its own railway halt in an effort to reduce hooliganism.

11 December
Elton watches Liverpool beat his Watford FC 3-1 in a league football match.

17 December
Elton arrives at the Xenon Club at 1am for a party to celebrate his first major concert tour for five years. He leaves 15 minutes later.

1983

MARCH
7 March
Elton records 'I Guess That's Why They Call It The Blues' in Montserrat.

9 March
Elton is interviewed on BBC *Breakfast Time*.

APRIL
30 April
Elton releases a new single titled 'I Guess That's Why They Call It The Blues'. The B-side, 'Choc Ice Goes Mental', is credited to Lord Choc Ice, a pseudonym for Elton. It reaches number 5 on the UK chart and Number 4 in the US.

MAY
12 May
Elton reveals plans for a joint tour with Rod Stewart for 1984.

Elton: "It's something we've been planning for some time. It won't be just the two of us on stage doing an hour each. We've been working together to produce a special show which will go on tour next summer".

The tour never happens.

19 May
Peter Duncan interviews Elton on *Blue Peter*.

27 May
Michael Wale interviews Elton on BBC *Nationwide*.

30 May
Elton arrives in Peking with Watford Football Club for a three-match tour of China.

JUNE
Elton releases a new album titled 'Too Low For Zero'. It reaches number 25 on the US chart.

23 June
Studio performance of 'I Guess That's Why They Call It The Blues' on *Top Of The Pops*.

26 June
Elton records 'I'm Still Standing' in Montserrat.

JULY
30 July
Elton releases a new single 'I'm Still Standing' backed with 'Earn While You Learn'. It reaches number 4 on the UK chart and Number 12 in the US.

AUGUST
23 August
The London *Evening News* reports that Elton's manager John Reid is in the running to become Rod Stewart's manager.

SEPTEMBER
14 September
The Sun reports on Rod Stewart's proposed tour with Elton, and talks to Rod: "I've been staying down at Elton's place at Ascot for a few days and we've been working very hard. Elton and I really are getting on like a house on fire. We have found that we sing in perfect harmony. This tour really is a big project for both of us. It's taking up almost all our time. We're going to be playing lots of great material that we have never done before - lots of old Motown and soul things. I'm starting a new album next month and then after that we'll be doing the tour. I hope we'll be coming to England next February."

26 September
Elton is interviewed on BBC *South Today*.

27 September
Rod Stewart cancels his projected tour with Elton, so that he can concentrate on recording a new album.

29 September
BBC *Breakfast Time*. Andrew Harvey visits Elton's home plus interview.

OCTOBER
15 October
'Kiss The Bride' backed with 'Dreamboat' is released as Elton's new single. It reaches number 20 on the UK chart and number 25 on the US chart.

31 October
The Daily Star reports that the plans for Elton and Rod Stewart to tour America and Britain next year, appearing together on stage for the first time since they were both struggling musicians in the Sixties, has been called off.

Elton: "It seems to be all off. I'm not very pleased about it. I don't know what's happening about it. We're supposed to be friends but I haven't heard from Rod for ages, he hasn't phoned me, but I've had a telex and it seems to be all off."

NOVEMBER
18 November
The Sun reports that Elton pulls out of a Hollywood charity show due to being severely ill with glandular fever.

DECEMBER
3 December
Noel Edmonds interviews Elton on *The Late Late Breakfast Show*. Elton performs 'Cold As Christmas'.

10 December
Elton is one of the guests in the studio on BBC TV's *Saturday Superstore*.
 'Cold As Christmas' backed with 'Crystal' is released as the new single. It reaches number 33 on the UK chart.

25 December
Elton performs 'Cold As Christmas' on *The Two Ronnies*.

26 December
Elton is interviewed on Radio One's *1983 - The Year That Was*.

29 December
Peter Duncan talks to Elton on *Blue Peter's* 'Review Of The Year'.

1984

FEBRUARY

14 February
St Valentine's Day. Elton marries Renate Blauel at St Marks Church in Darling Point, Sydney, Australia. A £100,000 reception at the Sebel Town House hotel follows. John Reid is Elton's best man.

19 February
Linda Sawford (née Woodrow) tells the *Sunday Mirror* how in the days when Elton was Reg Dwight - a struggling entertainer - he jilted her days before they were to marry.

24 February
A dozen anti-apartheid demonstrators today staged a protest outside the Auckland hotel where Elton is staying. They are angry over his decision last year to perform in Sun City, the South African casino resort. Elton and Renate are in Auckland this weekend for the last of three concerts he is giving in New Zealand at the start of his latest world tour.

MARCH
Dates: Sydney (24 & 25).

Elton tours Australia.

APRIL
Dates: Gdansk, Poland (5), Stockholm (30).

5 April
Elton winds up his Polish concert tour in Gdansk after concerts in Katowice and Warsaw. For the Gdansk concert, the Solidarity leader Lech Walesa is Elton's guest at the gig.

12 April
Interview with Elton on BBC *Sixty Minutes*.

Elton announces that Graham Taylor, manager of Watford FC, has signed a contract tieing him to the club for six years.

Elton: *"I can't say how delighted I am. It gives the club and the supporters a tremendous boost. The club will grow and grow under him. In a week leading up to the most important game in the club's history, it is the best news that the team could have."*

13 April
David Icke visits Watford football ground to interview Elton on BBC *Breakfast Time* about his chairmanship of Watford FC and their prospects in the FA Cup semi-final.

19 April
Elton records 'Sad Songs' in Montserrat.

20 April
The *Daily Mirror* reports that Elton, fresh back from his successful Australian tour, has bought a green and white Sydney tram complete with electrodes and which is now housed in the garden of his Windsor home.

MAY
Dates: Stuttgart (15).

10 May
Elton appears at the 24th Golden Rose of Montreux pop concert which is recorded for sale to broadcasting organisations round the world.

12 May
Elton sends a wreath to Diana Dors' funeral in Sunningdale, Berkshire.

19 May
Elton and Renate go to Wembley Stadium for the Cup Final between Watford and Everton. Elton tours the stadium in an open top vintage car with Everton chairman Philip Caffer in a bid to keep the peace between rival fans.

26 May
Elton releases a new single 'Sad Songs' backed with 'A Simple Man'. It reaches number 7 on the UK chart and number 5 in the US.

28 May
Elton performs 'Sad Songs' on BBC TV's edited highlights of the Montreux Golden Rose Pop Festival.

JUNE
Dates: Ludwigshaven (2), Sports Palace, Barcelona (9), Teatro Tendra, Milan (11 & 12), Kings Hall, Belfast (15), Dublin (16), Leeds (19), Edinburgh (26), Wembley Stadium, London (30).

5 June
Elton performs 'I Guess That's Why They Call It The Blues' on part two of BBC TV's edited highlights of the Montreux Golden Rose Pop Festival.

ELTON AND HIS BRIDE RENATE LEAVE ST MARK'S CHURCH AFTER THEIR WEDDING

30 June
Elton's Wembley Stadium Summer Concert '84 is broadcast on Radio One.

AUGUST
2 August
Elton films the video for the 'Passengers' single at St Tropez in the South of France, during his honeymoon.

8 August
Elton is interviewed on the *Travel Show* during his honeymoon in St Tropez while also filming his new video.

11 August
'Passengers' backed with 'Lonely Boy' is released as Elton's new single. It reaches number 5 in the UK chart.

SEPTEMBER
Dates: Houston, Tx (2), Alpine Valley (9), Maple Leaf Gardens, Toronto (13), St Paul, Minn (18), Kansas City, Ka (20), Houston, Tx (28)

OCTOBER
Dates: Omni, Atlanta, Ga (6), Madison Square Garden, New York (23-25), Spectrum, Philadelphia (29).

ELTON ON STAGE IN DUBLIN, JUNE 16 1984

11 October
Elton recovers after collapsing in his dressing room during his rigorous American tour. The illness, diagnosed as a virus infection, forces Elton to cancel the sell-out concert in Charlotte, North Carolina.

24 October
'Who Wears These Shoes?' backed with 'Tortured' is released as the new single. It reaches number 50 on the UK chart and number 16 on the US chart.

NOVEMBER
Dates: The Centrum, Worcester, Mass (3-5), Madison Square Garden, New York (12).

DECEMBER
16 December
Elton announces Torvill & Dean as winners of the BBC Sports Personality Of The Year Award on BBC TV.

25 December
Elton is one of the guests on *Wogan*.

1985

FEBRUARY

14 February
Elton releases a new single titled 'Breaking Hearts' for St. Valentine's Day and Elton's first wedding anniversary. It reaches number 59 on the UK chart.

18 February
Elton is interviewed on Radio One's *From Punk To Present* series. He mimes to 'Too Low For Zero' on *Wogan*.

23 February
Elton is music and phone-in guest on BBC TV's *Saturday Superstore*.

MARCH

13 March
Elton presents George Michael with the Best Songwriter Award at the annual Ivor Novello Ceremony at London's Grosvenor House.

15 March
BBC TV's *Friday People* interviews Elton at the Ivor Novello Ceremony.

29 March
BBC TV's *Friday People* interviews Elton.

APRIL

19 April
The Daily Star reports that Elton was summoned to take dinner at Windsor Castle with the Queen Mother and Princess Margaret. The purpose was to introduce his new wife Renate to his admiring Royal fans.

JUNE

2 June
Highlights from the 1985 Montreux Rock Festival feature Elton and Millie Jackson performing 'Act Of War'.

4 June
BBC News reports on Elton's visit to the High Court to sue his former manager Dick James for the return of copyright to many of his early songs.

10 June
BBC News reports on the concert which Bob Geldof is organising for Ethiopian famine relief, and interviews Elton who says,

"It is an outstanding achievement and it will be the concert of the decade."

Elton is interviewed at his home for *Blue Peter*.

15 June
'Act Of War' is released as the new single by Elton and Millie Jackson. It reaches number 32 on the UK chart.

22 June
Music Week reports that in the High Court last week Elton and Bernie Taupin claimed they had lost around £1 million in foreign royalties through money siphoned off by subsidiaries of Dick James Music.

28 June
Wembley Stadium. Elton duets with George Michael on 'Candle In The Wind' at Wham!'s farewell concert.

29 June
In a further report on the High Court case between Elton and the Dick James Organisation, *Music Week* states that the DJO had challenged Elton's claim that they "whittled away vast sums of money" that should have been his. Elton was confronted with sets of figures showing that while he earned more than £15.5 million from his songs up to December

ELTON WITH GEORGE MICHAEL AT THE 1985 IVOR NOVELLO AWARDS

WITH BOB GELDOF

WITH BOB GELDOF

OCTOBER

12 October
'Nikita' backed with 'The Man Who Never Died' is released as Elton's new single. It reaches number 3 on the UK chart and number 7 on the US chart.

Elton is live studio guest on Noel Edmond's *Late Late Breakfast Show*.

17 October
Live studio performance of 'Nikita' on *Top Of The Pops*.

18 October
Elton is studio 'Guest of the Day' on BBC *Breakfast Time*.

26 October
Music Week reports that the mammoth and massively expensive legal battle between Elton and publisher Dick James is entering its final stages, but such is the complexity of the action that a judgement may not be given until the New Year.

1982, DJM's labels made profits of £8.5 million. Elton said he could not comment. He and his lyric writing partner Bernie Taupin are suing Dick James and his companies, claiming the agreements signed with them 18 years ago were unfair and made under "undue influence". They want the contracts set aside and are seeking the return of copyrights they signed away for life, and damages. All their claims are contested by Dick James and the DJM Organisation.

JULY
Dates: Wembley Stadium (13).

6 July
Music Week reports that John Reid told the High Court last week how he called in accountants to audit DJM's sub publishing arrangements after becoming suspicious about the way Elton's songs were being published in the US. Reid said he believed the DJM subsidiary in New York was retaining too much of the money it collected in royalties. Reid began the inquiry just after leaving the Dick James

Organisation to independently manage Elton in 1972 - it continued over the next eight years until 1981 when writs were served on Dick James and his companies.

12 July
Elton is interviewed during final preparations for the Live Aid Concert.

13 July
The Live Aid Concert at Wembley Stadium, with a simultaneous live broadcast by BBC TV and Radio One. Elton performs 'I'm Still Standing', 'Bennie And The Jets', 'Rocket Man', 'Don't Go Breaking My Heart' (with Kiki Dee), and 'Don't Let The Sun Go Down On Me' (with George Michael).

AUGUST
10 August
Bernie Taupin asks *Music Week* to point out that he is still working with Elton following inaccurate information in which Taupin was described as Elton's *former* lyricist.

30 August
The Daily Express reports that Elton is planning to return to Russia next year. Secret negotiations have been going on between the Foreign Office and the Russians for Elton to take a big band to Moscow and Leningrad.

"Elton has always wanted to go back after his first tour there. He wants to play bigger places and to entertain more," says John Reid.

ON STAGE AT LIVE AID

ELTON ON STAGE WITH GEORGE MICHAEL DURING LIVE AID

"Elton John simply has never had a complaint about his career and about what was done for him in the way of exploitation and promotion. In fact, he is very fond of Dick James. He's grateful to him in many ways. He has amassed a considerable fortune because of what Dick James has done for him," says George Newman QC, barrister for Dick James.

NOVEMBER
Dates: RDS Stadium, Dublin (14-17), Newport Centre (20 & 21), St Austell, Coliseum (23 & 24), Sheffield, City Hall (26 & 27), Edinburgh, Playhouse (28 & 29).

7 November
'Wrap Her Up' is released as the new single by Elton and George Michael. The B-side is a live version of 'Restless'. The single reaches number 12 on the UK chart and number 20 on the US chart.

WITH QUEEN DRUMMER ROGER TAYLOR

WITH MILLIE JACKSON

WITH GEORGE MICHAEL AND ANDREW RIDGELEY AT LIVE AID

9 November

Elton joins Gladys Knight and Stevie Wonder on Dionne Warwick & Friends, AIDS fund raising single 'That's What Friends Are For'. It reaches number 16 on the UK chart and number 1 on the US chart.

14 November

Elton opens his UK tour at Dublin's RDS Stadium. His backing band comprises Davey Johnstone (guitar), David Paton (bass), Fred Mandel (keyboards), Ray Cooper (percussion) and Charles Morgan (drums). Backing vocalists are Alan Carvell, Shirley Lewis and Helena Springs, and also on stage are the Onward International Horns: Raul D'Oliviera and Paul Spong (trumpets), Rick Taylor (trombone) and David Bitelli (saxes).

16 November

Elton releases a new album 'Ice On Fire'.

25 November

Radio One broadcasts *Elton at the Beeb* concert.

27 November

Elton makes a donation to the Leukaemia Society during Ian Botham's sponsored walk from John O'Groats to Land's End. Interview with Elton on BBC *Breakfast Time*.

DECEMBER

Dates: Manchester, Apollo (1-3), Nottingham, Royal Concert Hall (4 & 5), Brighton Centre (7), Wembley Arena (11-19), Birmingham NEC (21-23), Bournemouth (30 & 31).

7 December

Music Week reports that Elton and Bernie Taupin last week narrowly failed in their bid to get a High Court decision that would have turned the industry on its head. The songwriting partnership were suing Dick James Music for the return of copyrights - estimated to be worth £30 million - for all their songs written between 1967 and 1975.

They claimed the original contracts had been signed under "undue influence". Had they succeeded in the action, DJM Managing Director Stephen James had said that it would be "the end of the music industry, as we know it". Elton and Taupin did win a secondary claim, however, for the repayment of foreign royalties siphoned off by overseas sub publishing arms of DJM.

11 December

Elton plays Wembley Arena during his Ice On Fire tour. His band comprises Davey Johnstone, David Paton, Fred Mandel, Ray Cooper and Charlie Morgan. Backing vocalists are Alan Carvell, Shirley Lewis and Helena Springs. also featuring on the tour is a brass section called the Onward International Horns.

13 December

The Daily Telegraph reports that the measure of Elton's public adoration can be seen by looking up at the huge sign above the entrance to Wembley Arena which says 'The Elton John Concerts Dec 11-19'. This is a 7000 seat venue and it's sold out on each of these nights.

15 December

Elton in concert at Wembley Arena on Radio One.

19 December

George Michael and Rod Stewart make a guest appearance at Elton's Wembley Arena concert.

1986

JANUARY
Dates: Glasgow Centre (3 & 4), Newcastle- upon-Tyne City Hall (5-7), Belfast Kings Hall (9-11).

29 January
Elton and Bernie Taupin are awarded £5 million in back royalties from Dick James Music, after lengthy and bitter court case.

FEBRUARY
Elton shocks the music industry as he walks out of the BPI Awards in London after receiving a belated Award from Norman Tebbit for his tour of Russia. He complains it was ridiculous that he had been given an award for something he had done seven years before.

4 February
Dick James dies in St Johns Wood following a heart attack.

8 February
Elton is special guest on *The Muppet Show.*

10 February
Elton receives Award for Outstanding Achievement for visit to Russia at the British Record Industry Awards. BBC live broadcast includes clips of Elton in Russia.

12 February
The Daily Star reports that Elton dismisses Britain's annual rock and pop awards as 'a joke'.

Elton: *"I will never go again, it's a load of rubbish. I don't know why they have awards. The only reason I can think of is that it makes good television - otherwise it's worthless."*

24 February
Elton appears on the BBC 1 chat show *Wogan.* He is interviewed and sings 'Cry To Heaven'.

26 February
The Daily Star reports how Elton revealed details of his private life to millions of French TV viewers during a programme called *The Truth Game* in which he hit back at rumours that he used Renate to try to hide his gay feelings.

Elton: *"It was just that I met someone whom I liked a lot and wanted to marry her. It happened at a moment when I was tired of my old style of living."*

28 February
The Daily Telegraph reports that Elton has agreed to pay the legal costs of the late Dick James, his adversary in last year's multi-million pound royalties battle in the High Court.

MARCH
Dates: Madrid (1), Barcelona (4), Lille (18), Basel (25), Paris.

WITH BERNIE

1 March
'Cry To Heaven' backed with 'Candy By The Pound' is released as Elton's new single. It reaches number 47 on the UK chart.

APRIL
Dates: Berlin (1), Vienna (20), Rotterdam (24),

7 April
Elton breaks off from his European tour to fly into London to collect the prestigious Ivor Novello Award for outstanding services to British Music. He also receives an award for last year's best song 'Nikita'.

Elton: *"It's a real honour. I'm really lucky to be surrounded by such good songwriters"*

13 April
The *Sunday Mirror* reports that Michael Parkinson and his *Desert Island Discs* team cast away from Broadcasting House and sailed off to Elton's Windsor home to record their radio programme with the singer - an honour they denied even to Royalty.

JUNE
Dates: Wembley Arena (20)

20 June
Elton performs 'I'm Still Standing' at the Tenth Birthday Party of The Prince's Trust held at Wembley Arena. The concert is filmed and recorded for later release.

JULY
3 July
The *Daily Mail* reports that Elton considered suicide after revealing his homosexual love life. Elton told presenter Paula Yates of the Channel 4 rock show *The Tube,*

Elton: *"The gay business really hurt me a lot. I'd stopped touring after announcing that I was a homosexual and had nothing else to do. If I hadn't had Watford I might have become a very big casualty.*

"But I had to learn to take defeat well. If you take your seat at a football ground and 20,000 people are singing 'Elton John is a homosexual' you learn fairly quickly. In America, when I said I was gay in 1976, a lot of radio stations didn't play my records. I stopped touring

in '76 because I'd had enough. I didn't know what more I could do."

23 July
Elton (in ponytail hairstyle) and wife Renate are guests at the Royal Wedding at Westminster Abbey, London, of HRH Prince Andrew Duke Of York and Sarah Ferguson

AUGUST
Dates: Madison Square Garden, New York (11-14), Detroit, Mi (15), Sandstone Amphitheater, Kansas City, Ka (21), Minneapolis (22), Chicago (23), Civic Center, Hartford, Ct (29), Saratoga Springs, NY (30).

13 August
The *Daily Mail* reports that the Duke and Duchess of York are being credited by friends with having saved the shaky marriage of Elton and his wife Renate which was going through troubled times during Andrew and Sarah's engagement. Invitations from the couple to Windsor neighbours Elton and Renate to participate in the bachelor and hen parties, the pre-wedding ball at the Guards Polo Club and the ceremony at Westminster Abbey worked wonders.

23 August
The *Daily Express* reports that Elton and his wife Renate are inviting their new friends the Duke and Duchess of York to a

75

party by way of saying thanks for helping them save their shaky marriage. Elton is staging the romantic event at the Watford Football Club's ground on 18 October to show off the new West Stand.

SEPTEMBER
Dates: The Centrum, Worcester, Mass (6), Providence, RI (7), Philadelphia, Pa (8), Madison Square Garden, New York (13 &14), The Omni, Atlanta, Ga (16), Tallahassee, Fl (20), Tampa, Fl (21), Jerry Park, Montreal.

OCTOBER
Dates: Oakland Coliseum, Ca (3).

4 October
Elton releases a new single 'Heartache All Over The World' backed with 'Highlander'. It reaches number 45 on the UK chart.

17 October
Elton appears on BBC TV's *Terry Wogan Show* hosted by Esther Rantzen.

NOVEMBER
Dates: Brisbane (5), Melbourne (17).

5 November
Elton begins a 27 concert tour of Australia in Brisbane, followed by dates in Adelaide, Perth, Melbourne and Sydney. He is accompanied by his 13-piece band, as well as the entire 88-musician Melbourne Symphony Orchestra. The first half of each concert consists of an hour and a half of Elton with his band; after an interval the rear section of the stage is drawn back to reveal the orchestra.

For the orchestral section of the shows, Elton wore his 'Amadeus' outfit, complete with beauty spot and a white wig with black bow.

7 November
Elton releases a new studio album titled 'Leather Jackets'. Work on this album started in May with a first time visit to Wisseloord Studios in The Netherlands. Taking five months to complete, all the tracks were recorded and mixed in a 48-track digital studio and produced by Gus Dudgeon. Guests on the album include Roger Taylor, John Deacon, Shirley Lewis, Cliff Richard and Kiki Dee.

13 November
Jonathan King interviews Elton from Hawaiian island of Maui for his *Entertainment USA* series.

21 November
'Slow Rivers' is released as the new single by Elton and Cliff Richard. It reaches number 44 on the UK chart.

27 November
A further interview with Elton on *Entertainment USA*.

DECEMBER
Dates: Sydney Entertainment Centre (9-14).

Elton's Australian tour continues.

9 December
Elton collapses on stage during concert in Sydney, Australia.

14 December
On the final night of Elton's Australian orchestral tour at the Sydney Entertainment Centre, the concert is recorded for a double album and the show is televised live by ABC Television to an estimated audience of ten million. 'Candle In The Wind' together with 'Don't Let The Sun Go Down On Me', recorded live, is released as a single from the show.

25 December
Christmas Morning With Noel Edmonds comes live from British Telecom Tower, featuring a link up with Elton in Australia and Cliff Richard in Britain to sing 'Slow Rivers' as a duet.

28 December
England beat Australia in the 3rd Test at Sydney and Elton throws champagne over himself in the England dressing room.

1987

JANUARY

1 January
In *The Sun* Elton pays a remarkable tribute to Ian Botham.

Elton: *"It's not just Ian's cricket that I adore - it's his love of life, his generosity, his complete openness. Sometimes you feel like you want to strangle him when he does something outrageous, but the great attraction for me is his kindness and his love of people. I've only ever known one person like Botham and that was John Lennon."*

5 January
Elton enters a Sydney hospital for throat surgery, and some of the world tour concerts are cancelled.

6 January
Elton recovering from throat operation in a Sydney hospital.

8 January
Elton is given a clean bill of health after his throat operation. He is told not to speak for a while.

19 January
Time magazine reports that Elton is recovering from exploratory throat surgery which was performed after he collapsed on-stage during a concert near the end of a 27-date tour in Sydney, Australia. Doctors said a biopsy showed a non-malignant lesion. Elton cancels all his concerts for 1987.

FEBRUARY

22 February
Elton begins a libel action for huge damages against *The Sun* newspaper after it publishes allegations of his taking part in drugs and sex orgies with rent boy prostitutes.

25 February
The Sun makes further allegations that Elton is involved in a drugs and vice scandal.

26 February
Scotland Yard invites *The Sun* newspaper to supply details of gay sex and drugs allegations it has made against Elton and promises a full investigation.

More allegations appear in *The Sun* newspaper with the headline "Elton's Kinky Kicks".

27 February
The Sun calls Elton "a liar" after Elton denies the sex and drugs revelations.

The *Daily Mirror* reports, after two days of intensive investigations, that Elton was in New York on the date that *The Sun* newspaper claims that Elton attended an orgy at a friend's house in Berkshire, and calls *The Sun* allegation "a lie".

The Daily Star reports that Elton is suing *The Sun* newspaper for £20 million for its continuing allegations that he had sex with young boys.

MARCH
Elton and his wife Renate announce they have split up.

He re-signs with MCA in the US.

3 March
The Sun reports that Elton has laughed off their allegations about his sex and drugs life with young rent boys.

8 March
In a world exclusive interview Elton tells the *The Daily Star* that:

"I'm coming back to England - for my wife, for my future, and for my fans. I'm coming home to clear my name".

10 March
In an interview with The *Daily Mirror* Elton vows to go into the witness box to tell the real truth about his love life.

Elton: "No matter what happens I will go into court, swear on the Bible and tell the truth about everything. I'm going to nail the newspaper that wrote all those lies. They have got no chance. I'm going to do it to clear my name, not for the money."

20 March
Elton flys back to Britain from Los Angeles to begin his libel action against *The Sun*.

25 March
Elton's 40th birthday party is held at John Reid's home in Rickmansworth.

26 March
The Daily Mail reports that the Duke and Duchess of York joined jetsetters at Elton's 40th birthday party last night.

27 March
The Daily Mail reports that a convicted criminal gatecrashed Elton's 40th birthday party and chatted with the Duke and Duchess of York, and mingled with guests who included Phil Collins, Eric Clapton, Ringo Starr and George Harrison.

ELTON WITH ROD STEWART AND ALANA HAMILTON

28 March
Elton talks to *The Daily Star* about the separation from his wife Renate.

Elton: *"I'm relieved it's over and that everything's finally come out in the open. I'm happy I don't have to carry on living a lie. I got so fed up with having to fib about our marriage and say everything was rosy, when it wasn't - but what could I do? Renate and I couldn't do anything or go anywhere without being asked if our marriage was on the rocks. The pressure was horrendous. We both felt so persecuted.*

"Our lives were totally invaded. Now the air has been cleared, it's a real weight off my mind."

29 March
The News Of The World reports that Elton has turned to Royal pal Fergie for comfort as he prepares to announce his marriage is over.

30 March
The Sun reports that Elton has been taking advice on his broken marriage from his oldest friend, Lee Everett, the former wife of Kenny Everett.

APRIL
Elton appears at an AIDS benefit show in London - his first live show since his throat operation.

3 April
The Sun reports that vicious attacks and threats of violence have been made against members of the gay community interviewed by *The Sun* during the Elton investigations.

7 April
The *Daily Mirror* reports that Elton is stepping down as chairman of Watford FC after putting 10 years and nearly £3 million into the First Division club, but he's only willing to sell to someone who loves Watford as much as he does. Negotiations have already started and unless Elton changes his mind the deal will go through.

16 April
Elton's lawyers issue two further libel writs against *The Sun,* its editor and journalists - making 10 writs in all - and two against *The Daily Star,* its editor and journalists.

Elton is pictured on the front page of *The Sun* with the headline "Elton Porn Photo Shame". The newspaper claims they are in possession of a pornograph showing Elton having sex with a young man, which is, they claim "simply too disgusting to print in a family newspaper". Further allegations are featured over a two-page spread with the headline "Elton's Five Day Orgy".

17 April
More allegations about Elton's private life appear in *The Sun,* under the headline "I Ran Coke For Elton".

18 April
Millions of TV viewers hear Elton talk about his private life on Michael Parkinson's *One To One* ITV show.
"I believed him and hope the viewers did too. I enjoyed the show and so did Elton. In fact, I thought he was bloody marvellous, considering the pressure he is under. He is obviously deeply upset. He feels he has been unfairly treated by the newspapers - and by *The Sun* in particular. So do I. He's an old mate of mine, and a great mate. None of this nonsense is going to change that." - Michael Parkinson.

The Sun urges its readers to sit down tonight and watch Elton's performance on the *Michael Parkinson Show.* The newspaper claims that Elton is lying, stating that... "If you believe Elton, you'll believe in fairies".

WITH BERNIE

MAY

19 May

In an interview with the *Daily Mirror*, Elton thanks the *Mirror* for disproving allegations about rent boys.

Elton: "You helped the nation keep firmly on my side and I'm very grateful for that. It's been horrible, but now I'm back."

"I feel like I'm a kid again - I am totally rejuvenated. It has been the worst six months of my life. It has been a terrible time that I must now forget."

JUNE

3 June

Elton tells *The Daily Mail* that his voice is lower in pitch after a throat operation earlier this year.

Elton: "My voice is going to be fine but it needs rest. At one point about two months after the operation, I was very frightened, I wouldn't get any falsettos; I think that in timbre, my voice has gone down in pitch, but I've got my falsetto back. I plan to give my voice at least a year and a bit off. I did three or four years touring straight and I'm just taking a sabbatical at the moment to get my momentum back."

5 June

Elton is one of the guests on *Wogan*, and sings 'Flames Of Paradise' with Jennifer Rush.

9 June

Elton is interviewed on Jonathan King's *Entertainment USA 2* programme.

10 June

Elton and Jennifer Rush are interviewed on *BBC Breakfast Time*.

20 June

Elton is interviewed on Radio One's *Eric Clapton Story*.

JULY

A live version of 'Your Song' is released as Elton's new single.

5 July
Elton is interviewed on Radio One's *Eric Clapton Story*.

AUGUST
1 August
Elton is interviewed on Radio One's *Eric Clapton Story*.

18 August
Elton talks about the problems of the British Royal Family during a phone-in programme in Los Angeles.

Elton: *"It is a tragedy that Prince Charles could not become Sovereign immediately. The Prince and his lovely wife have captured the imagination of the young people in England. So many kids are facing no future. The Prince, through the Trust, is giving them opportunities they wouldn't otherwise have. I think it's a tragedy he can't become King".*

"I've always gotten on very well with the Prince - and his wife. Charles, unlike Diana, doesn't like to rock and roll."

24 August
Elton is interviewed and seen performing 'Back In The USSR' in Moscow on BBC TV's *The Rock'n Roll Years: 1979*.

SEPTEMBER
12 September
Elton releases his new album 'Live In Australia', a double live album recorded during his 1986 tour. It reaches Number 70 on the UK chart and Number 24 on the US chart.
  Geffen Records in America release 'Elton's Greatest Hits Vol.3'. It reaches number 84 on *Billboard*'s chart.

ELTON WITH JENNIFER RUSH

28 September

The Sun claims that Rottweiler dogs guarding the grounds of Elton's mansion have been silenced by an operation to stop them barking.

OCTOBER

1 October

The London *Evening Standard* reports that Elton has collected a top music award. He received the American Society of Composers, Authors and Publishers Golden Note Award to mark 20 years of songwriting.

NOVEMBER

4 November

Elton pledges £7,000 to a children's charity to stop wife Renate singing on stage with Bob Geldof, Jonathan Ross and other stars at a concert in London.

19 November

The Sun reports that Elton is winding down his record company because all his acts are flops. Rocket Records announces that contracts for its two remaining performers will not be renewed. Elton will continue to record for Rocket so the company will still exist in principal.

21 November

Robert Maxwell makes bid to take over Watford FC by buying Elton's share for £2 million.

28 November

Elton attends his last home match as Watford FC chairman before handing over to John Holloran of Robert Maxwell's company.

DECEMBER

Elton records 'I Don't Wanna Go On With You Like That' in London.

4 December

The Football League prevents Robert Maxwell completing his deal to buy Elton's controlling interest in Watford FC.

16 December

BBC News coverage reports that Elton still hopes that Maxwell will buy his shares in Watford FC.

19 December

Elton joins Mike Yarwood, Sue Barker, Emlyn Hughes, Sara Gomer and Annabel Croft at the Brighton Centre to play in Cliff Richard's Christmas pro-celebrity tennis tournament.

20 December

Maxwell withdraws from his attempt to buy control of Watford FC from Elton.

25 December

Christmas Morning with Noel Edmonds, live from Telecom Tower, London features a Christmas message from Elton.

Elton is the musical guest on *Christmas Night With The Two Ronnies* and sings 'Candle In The Wind'.

ELTON WITH THE WATFORD FC SQUAD

1988

JANUARY

12 January
Elton is quizzed by detectives from Scotland Yard's Vice Squad for three hours in the offices of his lawyer, in central London.

13 January
The Sun reports that Elton pledges:

"I won't sell Watford FC to any old riff-raff. I am not going anywhere and I will not be selling out to anyone. I will not be selling my soul to the devil".

16 January
A live version of 'Candle In The Wind' backed with a live version of 'Sorry Seems To Be The Hardest Word' is released as Elton's new single. It reaches number 5 on the UK chart.

FEBRUARY

5 February
The Sun reports that Elton is dropped from Michael Aspel's TV chat show at the last minute to allow more time for Liz Taylor, who suddenly agreed to answer questions from the Aspel & Company audience. TV chiefs immediately decide that Elton can wait until a later programme.

7 February
Civic Hall, Guildford. Elton and Phil Collins join Eric Clapton on stage.

MARCH

Elton throws a lavish 35th birthday party for Renate at Covent Garden's trendy night-club Brown's.

Re-promoted double album 'Live In Australia', without its boxed packaging reaches number 43 on the UK chart.

Elton stars in a TV commercial for Cadbury's chocolate called 'Chunky Bar Spectacular'. He also writes the music.

ELTON SMOOCHES WITH RENATE AT HER BIRTHDAY PARTY IN BROWNS RESTAURANT IN LONDON'S COVENT GARDEN.

11 March
The Daily Star reports that Elton is joining Ian Botham's "Hannibal" elephant walk across the Alps. Elton has told Botham that he would be delighted to take part in the mammoth trek later this month.

26 March
The Sun reports that Elton is re-recording an entire album after a studio blunder wiped out the master tape. Elton had taken three months to complete the songs during sessions in Los Angeles and has now been forced to postpone his return to Britain to do every song again.

APRIL
7 April
The Sun reports that Elton has flown to comfort his friend George Michael after illness nearly wrecked the young singer's first solo world tour. Elton jets from Los Angeles to visit George in Hawaii as he recovers from the throat infection and back injury which forced him to cancel four shows.

15 April
The Daily Star reports that Elton has made a half million pound promise to help Watford FC bounce straight back to Division One, by saying that his commitment to the Club will be as strong as ever - and has already proved it with hard cash.

MAY
'I Don't Wanna Go On With You Like That' backed with 'Rope Around A Fool' is released as the new single. It reaches number 30 on the UK chart.

21 May
The Daily Telegraph reports that Elton attempted to sell Watford FC to Robert Maxwell, the publishing magnate , in December, but was blocked by a Football League ruling banning chairmen from owning more than one club.

ON STAGE DURING THE PRINCES TRUST CONCERT AT WEMBLEY ARENA

Elton: *"In the last two weeks I have spent probably more time at the club than I have in the last two years and the spirit is magnificent. Therefore I plan to get involved, give them more money and give them something to fight for."*

JUNE

Dates: Royal Albert Hall, London (5,6).

2 June

The Sun reports that John Reid was fined £150 yesterday for his assault on *The Sun's* columnist Rick Sky on 16 May at an end of tour party for Whitney Houston.

6 June

The Prince and Princess of Wales join 4500 other pop music fans to help raise more than £2 million for underprivileged children at the Prince's Trust Gala held at the Royal Albert Hall. Elton is joined by Eric Clapton, Phil Collins, Midge Ure, Peter Gabriel, Rick Astley and The Bee Gees. BBC TV screen the concert on 23 June.

JULY

Dates: Los Angeles (8).

5 July

The Daily Express reports that Elton is to sell £3 million worth of his treasures at Sotheby's. Part of his art collection will be exhibited at the Victoria and Albert Museum in August together with memorabilia from his musical career, ranging from stage costumes to the outrageous fancy spectacles he has worn at concerts throughout the world.

8 July

The Daily Express reports that Elton has suddenly pulled out of Ken Russell's new film *The Rainbow* based on D H Lawrence's novel. Elton was to have played Uncle Henry, a flamboyant good-liver.

16 July

Elton releases a new studio album titled 'Reg Strikes Back'. It reaches number 11 on the UK chart and number 17 on the US chart.

AUGUST

7 August

The *Sunday Mirror* reports that Elton stormed off the set of his latest pop video because he had managed to record only TWO lines of his new single in TWELVE hours. A spokesman for Phonogram Records said "It was all arranged very quickly and the result was that filming was done almost as they went along. After 12 hours, they had shot only two lines of the song. He was as fed up as everyone else".

8 August

Elton puts most of his huge collection of pop and art memorabilia up for auction. Until this is sold at Sotheby's next month, some of the items go on display at the V & A. A BBC News report on the sale includes an interview with Elton.

The Daily Star reports that Elton looks set to play Liberace in a film version of the flamboyant pianist's life story which is to be made for American TV. All three networks are currently negotiating with the producers for screening rights.

Elton: *"It's time, artistically and mentally, for a change of thought. You cannot stagger through life with all these possessions. This is kind of like watching your own death. Hopefully I'll still be alive when the sale comes up in September."*

9 August

The display of Elton's art collection opens at the Victoria and Albert Museum in London, and runs until 23 August.

WITH PHIL COLLINS

10 August

The *Daily Mirror* reports that Elton has admitted he was worried about AIDS and had been tested for it many times. "The AIDS problem worries me. It should worry everyone. People ask me if I've ever had an AIDS test, well I have. I have blood tests all the time. The positive thing is awareness. People are being made not to panic."

SEPTEMBER

Dates: Miami, Fl (9 & 10), Tampa, Fl (11), Poplar Creek, Chicago, Ill (15-17), Marcus Amphitheater, Milwaukee, Wi (18), Madison Square Garden, New York, (19-23), Hollywood Bowl, Los Angeles, Ca (24 & 25).

3 September

Elton releases a new single titled 'Town Of Plenty' backed with 'Whipping Boy'. It reaches number 74 on the UK chart.

4 September

The News Of The World reports that Elton has asked his wife Renate for a divorce. The couple have lived virtually separate lives for months. Renate is flying home to Munich to break the news to her parents, while Elton is jetting off to the States.

6-9 September

Two thousand items from Elton's personal collection of memorabilia and antiques are auctioned at Sotheby's in London. The giant Pinball Wizard boots

from the *Tommy* film sell for £11,000 and dozens of other items from gold discs to personalised spectacles and original works of art by W. S. Lowry, René Magritte, Pablo Picasso and Andy Warhol, furniture by Carlo Bugatti, jewellery from Cartier and decorative lamps from the famous Tiffany workshop, contribute to a seven-figure sale.

The four glossy catalogues from the sale, in a slip-case, cost £60 and become a collector's item in themselves.

7 September

The Daily Mail reports that Elton is delighted with the sale of his old possessions at Sotheby's. The sale came about when he cleared out his Windsor mansion for re-decorating.

9 September

Elton's Reg Strikes Back American tour opens in Miami.

10 September

The *Daily Telegraph* reports that the sale of the Elton John Collection at Sotheby's raised £4,838,022 when the four-day sale ended last night. High estimate for the sale beforehand was £3 million. Sotheby's added the Elton John banners hanging outside their front door as extra lots at the end of the sale, and obtained £550 each for them.

23 September

Elton concludes five sell-out performances supported by Wet Wet Wet at New York's Madison Square Garden. His final concert breaks The Grateful Dead's career record of 25 sell-out Madison Square Garden concerts.

This is the opening night of a work tour on which his backing band comprises Davey Johnstone (guitar), Fred Mandel and Guy Babylon (keyboards), Romeo J. Williams (bass) and Jonathan Moffett (drums). Back-up singers are Marlena Jeter, Mortonette Jenkins and Natalie Jackson.

THE BOOTS WORN BY ELTON DURING HIS 'PINBALL WIZARD' SEQUENCE IN THE TOMMY MOVIE

25 September

Eric Clapton joins Elton on stage at the Hollywood Bowl for 'Saturday Night's Alright For Fighting'.

OCTOBER

Dates: Hartford Civic Center (7), The Centrum, Worcester (9), The Palace, Detroit, Mi (12-15), Madison Square Garden, New York (17-18 & 20-22).

Elton produces and writes for Olivia Newton-John's new album titled 'The Rumour'.

Eric Clapton undertakes a special four-date tour of Japan with Mark Knopfler and Elton. One concert at the Tokyo Dome is later broadcast on Japanese radio and television.

ELTON, RENATE AND RINGO STARR

13 October
Elton tells David Wigg for his *Daily Express* pop exclusive of the year:

"Life became like a James Bond movie. But you can't live your life a prisoner and hiding from everyone. You just have to be yourself. I used to hate the name Reg Dwight. I was unhappy with it as a kid, but now I'm older it's time to own up. I was born Reg and I am Reg. I feel comfortable with that now. I don't want to live a fantasy life as Elton John. I'm very happy with my own personality. I can be very normal or I can be completely off the wall. That's how I've become."

NOVEMBER
Dates: The Stadium, Osaka, Japan (5).

Elton releases 'A Word In Spanish' backed with 'Heavy Traffic' as his new single.

5 November
The Stadium, Osaka, Japan. Elton tours as part of Eric Clapton's band. Also on board are Mark Knopfler on guitar, Steve Ferrone on drums, Ray Cooper on percussion, Nathan East on bass, Alan Clark on keyboards and Katie Kisson and Tessa Niles on backing vocals. Songs by Elton in the set include 'Candle In The Wind', 'I Guess That's Why They Call It The Blues', 'I Don't Wanna Go On With You Like That', 'I'm Still Standing', 'Daniel', 'Saturday Night's Alright For Fighting'.

17 November
A press announcement confirms that Elton and Renate are to divorce. Although the exact figure is not disclosed, rumours suggest Renate's settlement could be any figure between £3 and £25 million.

18 November
Elton's wife Renate speaks to *The Daily Express* about their plans to divorce. "I am obviously saddened. I wish Elton all the happiness in the world, and I know he wishes me the same. We are both confident that all personal matters will be resolved without any animosity. Both of us have been, and will be, so busy with our own working commitments that we are seeing too little of each other, and for this reason it seems that we are unavoidably growing apart. We are however parting on the most amicable terms and genuinely intend to remain best friends."

20 November
Elton tells *The Mail On Sunday* of his sadness and guilt at the end of his marriage to Renate.

"Of course it's sad. I gave it my best shot. And it's certainly not Renate's fault. She's done nothing wrong. That's what makes it so hard. I feel this terrible guilt. She was so supportive when things were going badly for me. She was absolutely wonderful, and I hate any disruption to people I like. We had some really good times. There are people who won't believe this but it is all amicable. We don't feel any malice - quite the reverse in fact.

89

"The worst part is thinking that we might hurt each other, which is very easy to do when you love each other. Parting was a very painful decision to make."

27 November
In an exclusive interview with *The Mail On Sunday,* Elton talks about depression, food and drink.

Elton: *"It was near enough a nervous breakdown. I was, in fact, mentally unstable. I couldn't go out of the house without breaking down in tears. That's the reason I couldn't go to see football matches. Couldn't go anywhere. I tried being positive. Told myself to stop feeling so sorry for myself.*

Come on, pull yourself together. And it didn't work. So I went into hiding. Just didn't see the point of making a spectacle of myself in public. And that failure upset me .

"I started eating six times what I should have done, and that depressed me too. I've always been a very emotional person, but this was different...

"At one point, early this year, I started drinking vodka martinis. I was particularly addicted to them. You're supposed to sip them, but I'm an all or nothing person and I just used to whoosh them back. I got to the stage where I was drinking 10 or

18 martinis a day. I would need three or four before I went out in the evening. Then I'd go on to red wine. Getting older, you learn more. You have to face the fact that you must clean up your act if necessary. I enjoy it. You get more out of life."

DECEMBER
1 December
The Post reports that Elton could make his first public appearance since the break-up of his marriage at a Christmas benefit concert for AIDS sufferers. *The Post* exclusively reveals that Billy Connolly has invited Elton to appear as one of the guests at a concert to raise funds for Scottish kids with the disease and other AIDS charities. Connolly is to host the event at London's Strand Theatre on 11 December.

12 December
Elton is pictured on the front page of *The Sun* with the headline "Sorry Elton". *The Sun* agrees to pay Elton £1 million libel damages. The settlement followed allegations published in *The Sun* last year about his private life.

A delighted Elton says:

"This is the best Christmas present I could wish for. Life is too short to bear grudges and I didn't bear **The Sun** *any malice".*

A *Sun* spokesman apologises to Elton for running stories which they acknowledge to be completely untrue.

"We are delighted *The Sun* and Elton have become friends again, and are sorry that we were lied to by a teenager living in a world of fantasy."

13 December
The Sun reports that Elton claims that the British record charts are fixed. In an interview, Elton says:

"I am totally perplexed by some of the things that happen in the Top 40. There has to be something wrong with a situation where a record can come straight into the charts one week at number two drop down the Top 10 the next week then vanish into the twenties. It's a joke. Compare that with the States where it takes 20 weeks for a record to make its way up the charts and any record company that tells you otherwise is lying. There is no logic to some of the things that happen. I find the whole scene in the charts very surprising."

1989

FEBRUARY

15 February
Elton jives with the Queen at Buckingham Palace to Bill Haley's 'Rock Around The Clock'.

MARCH
Dates: Lyons, France (20), Bercy Stadium, Paris (22-27).

17 March
The Daily Star reports that Elton has just spent £4.5 million to buy the world's most exclusive bachelor pad in one of the most expensive streets in Florida's Palm Beach.

20 March
Elton begins his world tour in Lyons. The tour will encompass 12 European countries - France, Belgium, Germany, Denmark, Sweden, Norway, Switzerland, Spain, Italy, Austria, the UK and Ireland.

The band for this tour comprises Davey Johnstone on guitars, Fred Mandel and Guy Babylon on keyboards, Romeo Williams on bass, Jonathan Phillip Moffett on drums, and Marlena Jeter, Natalie Jackson and Mortonette Jenkins on vocals.

23 March
The Daily Express reports that Elton yesterday launched himself into a punishing world tour in Paris. It will take him to more than 30 countries with audiences topping 2,300,000 people.

24 March
Elton collapses on stage in front of 16,000 fans. His show comes to a dramatic halt when he fainted at the Bercy Stadium in Paris. Elton keeled over during an energetic dance routine and a doctor was called. A French production assistant said, "Apparently his blood pressure suddenly dropped. It was terribly hot and there was a huge crowd out there". After a few minutes Elton was revived and went back on stage to delight fans by continuing his concert.

27 March
Elton celebrates his 42nd birthday with a £200,000 party in Paris.

APRIL
Dates: Stockholm (9), Lausanne (19), Milan (27).

4 April
The Independent reports that the Press Council tells *The Daily Star* to remedy an inaccurate story about Elton spending £4.5 million on a mansion in Palm Beach, Florida, and a second article run the next day reported that Elton had denied suggestions that he planned to leave Britain.

MAY
Dates: Stadthalle, Vienna (1), Zurich (5), Birmingham NEC (17-19), Wembley Arena (22-25 & 27-30).

17 May
Elton opens the British leg of his world tour at Birmingham NEC. Support is Nik Kershaw.

24 May
Cathy McGowan interviews Elton for pop slot on *Newsroom South East.*

JUNE
Dates: Edinburgh Playhouse (1 & 2), Belfast, Kings Hall (5 & 6), Dublin, RDS Stadium (8-10).

5 June
Elton takes part in *Our Common Future* global broadcast to draw attention to the crisis which threatens the world environment.

JULY
Dates: Providence, RI (29).

29 July
Elton begins his tour of the US and Canada, covering 54 cities. This is part of the world tour.

AUGUST
Performing Center, Greatwoods (1&2), Meadowlands, NJ (4-7), Sandstone Amphitheater, Kansas City, Ka (12), San Francisco (20), Poplar Creek, Chicago (26 &27), Cuyahuga Falls, Ohio (29).

Elton releases a new album titled 'Sleeping With The Past'. It reaches number one in the UK chart.

19 August
The Daily Telegraph comments that Elton is an exceptional character who has diligently helped to build a friendly club at Watford with a pleasant atmosphere. He has nursed Watford FC from the Fourth Division to the First.

24 August
Elton sings 'Pinball Wizard' during an all star charity performance of The Who's rock opera *Tommy* at the Universal Amphitheater in Los Angeles. As well as Roger Daltrey, Pete Townshend and John Entwistle of The Who, also taking part are Steve Winwood, Phil Collins, Patti Labelle and Billy Idol.

26 August
'Healing Hands' backed with 'Dancing In The End Zone' is released as Elton's new single. It reaches number 45 on the UK chart.

28 August
Elton appears on BBC TV's *Terry Wogan Show*. He is the only guest on this special Bank Holiday edition.

SEPTEMBER
Dates: Pipe Knob, Detroit, Mi (1-3), The Omni, Atlanta, Ga (16 &17), Spectrum, Philadelphia, Pa (30).

OCTOBER
Dates: Madison Square Garden, New York, USA (3-7), Orlando, Fla (14), New Haven, Ct (18), Royal Albert Hall, London (31).

7 October

Eric Clapton joins Elton on stage at this Madison Square Garden concert for 'Rocket Man'.

The Daily Star reports that Elton has been ordered to rest after collapsing just hours before his farewell American show. He keeled over with exhaustion for the third time this year at the end of his gruelling 62 date tour. Now Elton has taken off to Paris for a big break before the next concert of his year-long world tour in South America.

8 October

Elton releases a new single 'You Gotta Love Someone' backed with 'Medicine Man'. It reaches Number 33 on the UK chart.

16 October

Interview with Elton on Jonathan King's *Entertainment USA*.

22 October

The News Of The World reports how Elton has redesigned his looks, his life and his music.

Elton: *"The most important thing for me is trying to be happy within myself. What I do as a profession is very important to me as well. But I think that for any individual, more than anything, if your job overtakes your life, that's very dangerous. I love doing what I do and I am very privileged to be able to do it. But I still think my personal life is far more important to me than any stagecraft or the records I make."*

28 October

The Sun reports that Elton, after a disastrous US tour in which he pulled out of three concerts, hopes to beat his nervous exhaustion by taking a complete break at the luxurious Ritz in Paris.

Elton: *"To say I collapsed is absolutely ridiculous. I am not seriously ill – I'm just plain tired. It's been a great tour but it all caught up with me. I wanted to give my best and that wasn't possible. Rather than disappoint anyone, I decided to cancel the concert."*

NOVEMBER

The world tour continues as Elton begins his tour of South East Asia including Australasia, Singapore, Malaysia, Thailand, Japan and Hong Kong.

17 November

The Sun reports that Elton has pulled out of a pop festival still suffering from the exhaustion that ruined his American tour. Elton was due to top the bill at the Diamond Awards Festival, Antwerp, Belgium but has been forced to cancel the trip.

WITH ERIC CLAPTON, PROMOTING THEIR JOINT CONCERTS IN 1992

1990

JANUARY
More world tour dates in South America, including Chile, Argentina, Uruguay and Brazil.

FEBRUARY
Dates: Melbourne (1,2 & 3), Hobart (6 & 7).

MARCH
The world tour draws to a close after dates in Eastern Australia, NewZealand and Tasmania.

The *Daily Mirror* reports that Elton is to top the bill at a two-night concert extravaganza marking the launch of financially troubled tycoon Donald Trump's latest pleasure palace.
The American property mogul spent £400 million on building the lavish Taj Mahal complex which houses the world's biggest casino in Atlantic City, New Jersey.

APRIL
12 April
Indianapolis, USA. Funeral of Ryan White. Service includes Elton singing 'Candle In The Wind'. White, a haemophiliac, died of AIDS.

15 April
The News Of The World reports that John Reid is fighting back to health after being treated for the effects of cocaine and alcohol. He spent three days in a detox-ification unit at the Cedars Sinai medical centre in Los Angeles.

MAY
Dates: Beverly Hilton (8), Atlantic City , NJ (18-20).

8 May
Elton performs with Little Richard at the Lupus Foundation of America Annual Fundraising Gala at the Beverly Hilton in Beverly Hills.

26 May
Elton attends Bernie Taupin's 40th bithday party at The Roxbury Restaurant in Beverly Hills.

WITH LITTLE RICHARD

JUNE
Dates: Knebworth Park (30).

15 June
Elton is one of the guests on *Wogan*.

22 June
Elton performs 'Sacrifice' live on *Top Of The Pops*. After all this time, it is his first solo number one hit in the UK.

30 June
Knebworth. Elton plays in supergroup with Mark Knopfler and Eric Clapton.

Elton: *"I've done two world tours and albums non-stop. I finished Australia in March and that's the last thing I've done performing wise, apart from Knebworth. You know, I'm quite fed-up with performing at the moment as far as tours are concerned. I like to go on to challenging situations. The greatest thing you can do is perform live."*

AUGUST
6 August
BBC *South Today* reports and interviews Elton on his plan to back a play written by a 16 year old schoolboy from Hove, East Sussex. *It's Hard To Be Different* is about a teenager who contracts AIDS and is written by Stephen McAlindon.

SEPTEMBER
13 September
The Daily Express reports that John Reid is locked in lengthy meetings with his lawyers after newspaper stories alleging that Elton is an alcoholic, although for the past year, Elton has been getting himself into shape on tour with daily work-outs in hotel gyms.

NOVEMBER

24 November

Elton is studio guest on BBC TV's *Going Live.*

DECEMBER

15 December

Elton's 25th anniversary as a recording artist is celebrated in the US by the release of a four CD and four cassette box set titled 'To Be Continued'. No better summary of Elton's career is available. There are several rarities among the 68 tracks, such as 'Come Back Baby', his début composition, and the début single by Bluesology, the original 1970 version of 'Grey Seal' and 'Donner Pour Donner', a solo demo of 'Your Song', live versions of 'I Feel Like A Bullet' and 'Carla'/'Etude' and three more July 1990 recordings: 'Made For Me', 'I Swear I Heard The Night Talkin'' and 'Easier To Walk Away'. The set is not released in the UK.

Elton releases a new single 'Easier To Walk Away' backed with 'I Swear I Heard The Night Talkin''. It reaches number 63 on the UK chart.

WITH BILLY JOEL

A personal instructor has been helping to reduce weight caused by the good life. Friends insist he has never been a heavy drinker. However, this has not stopped him being accused of joining Alcoholics Anonymous to conquer a drink problem.

16 September

Elton is pictured on the front cover of *The Mail On Sunday's* You magazine, and in the feature pays tribute to Ryan White, the teenage boy he 'adopted' in America, and whose AIDS death launches Elton's own crusade against the killer disease.

Commenting on *The Sun* court case, Elton stated:

"I don't feel bitter about it. I speak to **The Sun.** *That's all been and gone. It's past. So many people go through life harbouring grudges and I don't want to do that. They paid me the money, most important they gave me the front page to publish a retraction. I still object to some of the things they do, the language they use, but it's got a little better."*

1991

JANUARY
27 January
The *Sunday Mirror* reports that Elton is attending Alcoholics Anonymous meetings in West Hollywood, California, and tells the 75 people present: "I am Elton - I am an alcoholic."

FEBRUARY
11 February
Elton appears at the 1991 British Record Industry Awards at the Dominion Theatre in London.

APRIL
1 April
During the first night of Rod Stewart's Wembley gigs, Elton joins Rod on stage wearing a black and gold frilly dress, stockings, high heels and a blonde wig. Whilst Rod sings 'You're In My Heart', Elton sits on his knee and serves him brandy from a silver tray. The prank was set up as an April Fool's joke by Rod's management.

MAY
17 May
Elton unveils a plaque to start building work on a new Out-Patients' clinic at Kings College Hospital.

JUNE
28 June
Elton presents Rod Stewart with the Nordoff Robbins Silver Clef award at a ceremony in London. Rod also makes an impromptu award to Elton when he gets his wife, Rachel, to hand him a music box with the inscription: "To my dear Sharon, my left leg has never been the same - love Phyllis."
It is a reference to the April Fool's joke Rods' management played on Rod earlier in the year.
Rod comments: "I've bought Elton a music box and I paid a lot for the fucking thing. I thought, it's a long time since Elton got his hand on a big box."

SEPTEMBER
5 September
Hutchinson publish a new biography of Elton written by Philip Norman. Simply titled Elton, it is published in hardback only.

OCTOBER
14 October
'Two Rooms', a tribute album of cover versions of John/Taupin compositions is released. Among the artists featured are Eric Clapton, The Who, Kate Bush, Sinéad O'Connor, Rod Stewart, Sting and Bon Jovi.

Eric Clapton: "I felt that I could identify with 'Border Song', it reminds me of when I first met Elton - I could feel a way of doing it; with a horn section in a bluesy kind of way. Everything I have ever heard Elton and Bernie write has moved me at the time - moved me, encouraged me and inspired me - everything."

31 October
Elton is interviewed on *Newsroom South East* about his past and present relationship with Watford FC.

NOVEMBER

Recording sessions for 'The One' album in Paris. These sessions run between now and March 1992.

'Don't Let The Sun Go Down On Me' is released as the new single by Elton and George Michael, with all proceeds donated to the Terrence Higgins Trust. The single reaches number 1 on the UK chart.

Elton: *"I told him not to put it out because I didn't think it was going to be a hit. I said 'George, this is a very crucial time for you. You've had this album out which hasn't been as successful as the "Faith" album, maybe you should think twice about putting a live single out'. I left that on his answering machine and he phoned back and said 'No, it's going to be fine'. Then of course it was number 1 in every country in the world. I thought it was a good record and everything, but I was worried about his career. Ha, just take care of your own Elton, he's doing fine."*

25 November
Elton introduces a BBC TV tribute to Freddie Mercury of Queen who died of AIDS the previous night.

Elton: *"Quite simply, he was one of the most important figures in rock'n'roll in the last 20 years."*

27 November.
Elton attends Freddie Mercury's funeral at the West London Cemetery in Kensal Green.

AT THE 1992 FREDDIE MERCURY BENEFIT CONCERT AT WEMBLEY STADIUM

WITH AXL ROSE

WITH SYLVESTER STALLONE

WITH IGGY POP

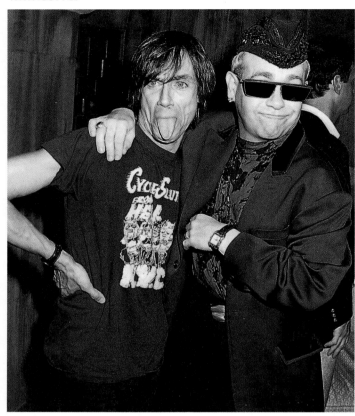

1992

JANUARY
15 January
Dee Murray, bass player in the original Elton John Band, dies at his home in Nashville, aged 45.

FEBRUARY
Elton stars in a controversial television commercial for Coca Cola. The 60 second ad features Elton singing and playing the piano and excerpts from films starring Humphrey Bogart, Louis Armstrong and other celebrities from bygone days.

MARCH
Dates: Carnegie Hall, New York, USA (12).

12 March
This concert is to help save rain forests. Also appearing are Natalie Cole, Don Henley, James Taylor and Sting.

DON HENLEY, JAMES TAYLOR, STING, TRUDY STYLER, NATALIE COLE AND ELTON

APRIL
Dates: Wembley Stadium (20)

20 April
This concert is the Freddie Mercury Tribute at Wembley. Appearing towards the end of the concert, Elton bravely tackles 'Bohemian Rhapsody' and duets with Axl Rose of Guns N' Roses on the song's HM coda and 'The Show Must Go On'. Elton's contribution subsequently appears on the video and live album from the event.

Elton: "I, Elton John, am not an exciting performer per se any more. I was when I was younger, but those days of doing headstands on the piano are gone. Axl is exciting, though. You need energy and he provided it."

MAY
Dates: Spektrum, Oslo (26&27), Stockholm Stadium (29&30), Osterbro Stadium, Copenhagen (31).

26 May
Elton starts his world tour in Oslo. The tour will eventually encompass 150 concerts world wide, drawing to a close towards Nîmes at the end of 1993.

The band for this tour consists of Davey Johnstone (guitar), Charlie Morgan (drums), Guy Babylon and Mark Taylor (keyboards), Bob Birch (bass), Natalie Jackson, Mortonette Jenkins and Marlena Jeter (backing vocals).

The set contains the following: 'Don't Let The Sun Go Down On Me', 'I'm Still Standing', 'I Guess That's Why They Call It The Blues', 'Tiny Dancer', 'Philadelphia Freedom', 'Burn Down The Mission', 'Simple Life', 'The One', 'Mona Lisas And Mad Hatters', 'Sorry Seems To Be The Hardest Word', 'Daniel', 'Blue Avenue', 'The Last Song', 'Funeral For A Friend/Love Lies Bleeding', 'Sad Songs', 'The Show Must Go On', 'Saturday Night's Alright For Fighting', 'Sacrifice', 'Song For Guy/Your Song'.

Elton's first tour for three years, with stage and costumes designed by none less than the *haute couture* giant Gianni Versace, and a souvenir video instead of a programme.

Elton: "It's going to be real fun. In the past I've said that I haven't meant it, but this time I'm looking forward to it and got physically fit for it. I wasn't in shape for the last tour - I hadn't been in shape for years and years and years - but now I play with a tennis pro for an hour and a half every morning, and I don't mess around. All the money I'm saving on the excessive things I used to do I'm putting into health things!"

JUNE
Dates: Dortmund Westfalenhalle (1, 2), Frankfurt Festhalle (4), Rock am Ring (6), Bremen Weser Stadium (7), Olympia Hall, Munich (9, 10, 12), Prater Stadion, Vienna (13), Berlin Waldbuhne (15,16), Les Arenes, Nîmes (17), Hippodrome de Vincennes, Paris (18), Feyenoord, Rotterdam (19), Sheffield Arena (21, 22), Wembley Stadium (26, 27, 28), NEC, Birmingham (30).

3 June
The Sun reports that Elton has scrapped interviews for his world tour after being badly let down by his biographer Philip Norman, who apparently sold a private conversation as a straightforward interview to *The Sunday Times* Magazine and a US magazine. During the chat over tea and sandwiches at his new Holland Park home, Elton revealed details about his booze and drugs past, and his new boyfriend.

11 June
Milan. A storm brings down a marquee at an AIDS benefit concert with Sting. Guests included Sylvester Stallone and Eric Clapton.

Elton: "I have never seen one like it, it was very frightening."

12 June
Elton John Day on Radio One includes an exclusive interview with Steve Wright.

15 June
Elton releases a new album titled 'The One'. The WH Smith chain of record stores in the UK offer a signed copy for the first person to buy it.

18, 19, 26, 27 & 28 June
These concerts are with Eric Clapton sharing top billing alongside Elton.

29 June
The Guardian review the Elton/Clapton concert at Wembley Stadium with the headline "Pop Kings Who Lost Their Fizz".

JULY

Dates: Forêt Nationale, Brussels (1), Lausanne, Pontaise Stadium (3), Basel, St Jakob Stadium (4), Bologna, Stadio Communale (6), Olympico, Rome (8), Monza, Stadio Brianteo (10), Nimes Open Air Arena (11), Plaza de Toros, Madrid (13), Seville Betis Stadium (15), Lisbon Stadium (16), Oviedo, Stadium (18), La Corunna Real Coliseum (19).

3, 4, 6, 8 & 10 July

More concerts with Eric Clapton sharing top billing with Elton.

25 July

BBC 2 TV screen edited highlights from Elton's concert in Barcelona.

Elton: *"This is going to sound terribly corny but I notice simple things in life now that I never did before.*

"The trees, the flowers, everything. I still live a complicated lifestyle, but I was all outside and no inside before. What you saw was what you got but inside was something totally different. Now my insides are happy, and I feel refreshed and ready to start again."

AUGUST

'Runaway Train' backed with 'Understanding Women' is released as Elton's new single.

24 August

In his first interview for three years Elton summons up the courage to acknowledge the lasting hurt he caused the loyal wife he drove away.

Elton: *"Even though I knew I was gay, I thought this woman was attractive and that being married would cure me of every- thing wrong in my life, and there's no doubt that my wife did love me, but it didn't change my way of life. I wasn't a sexual philanderer during that time but I certainly didn't stop taking drugs and alcohol and when you take that amount, you can't have any relationship. We finally ended up in this big house with separate bedrooms, never seeing each other. It was very sad ...the simple fact was that I wasn't being honest."*

John Reid: "He's much more aware of what's going on around him, and he's taking more time to enjoy things. He's not so wrapped up in himself, solely. And he's enjoying it all. What used to happen is that he'd set himself a goal, whether it was realistic or not, go for it - and then find he wasn't enjoying it. Certainly he's more calm. All the volatile behaviour has gone and it's quite a pleasure. The American photo- grapher Herb Ritts came to a gig last night and said 'Where's all the chaos?' because backstage it was just nice and pleasant. It's quite funny for people who have known him for a long time to be faced with this complete overhaul!"

1993

FEBRUARY/MARCH
Elton tours Australia, including
an extensive run in Melbourne
(February 16, 17, 19 & 20).

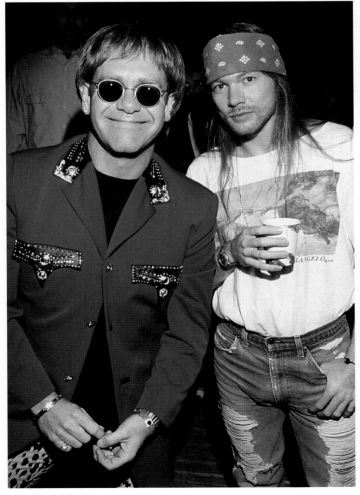

ELTON JOHN UK DISCOGRAPHY

SINGLES

Come Back Baby/Times Getting
Tougher Than Tough
Fontana TF 594, July 1965
(With Bluesology)

Mr Frantic/Everyday (I Have The Blues)
Fontana TF 668, February 1966 (With
Bluesology)

Since I Found You Baby/Just A Little Bit
Polydor 56195, October 1967 (With
Stu Brown & Bluesology)

I've Been Loving You/Here's To The
Next Time
Philips BF 1643, March 1968

Lady Samantha/All Across The Heavens
Philips BF 1739, January 1969

The Dick Barton Theme/Breakdown
Blues
Decca F 12891, February 1969 (With
The Bread And Beer Band)
Reissued on Decca F 13354, November
1972

It's Me That You Need/Just Like Strange
Rain
DJM DJS 205, May 1969

Border Song/Bad Side Of The Moon
DJM DJS 217, March 1970

Rock And Roll Madonna/Grey Seal
DJM DJS 222, June 1970

Your Song/Into The Old Man's Shoes
DJM DJS 233, January 1971

Friends/Honey Roll
DJM DJS 244, April 1971

Rocket Man/Holiday Inn/Goodbye
DJM DJX 501, April 1972

Honky Cat/It's Me That You Need/Lady
Samantha
DJM DJS 269, August 1972

Crocodile Rock/Elderberry Wine
DJM DJS 271, October 1972

Daniel/Skyline Pigeon
DJM DJS 275, January 1973

Saturday Night's Alright For Fighting/
Jack Rabbit/Whenever You're Ready
DJM DJX 502, June 1973

Goodbye Yellow Brick Road/Screw
You
DJM DJS 285, September 1973

Step Into Christmas/Ho! Ho! Ho!
DJM DJS 290, November 1973

Candle In The Wind/Bennie And The
Jets
DJM DJS 297, February 1974

Don't Let The Sun Go Down On Me/
Sick City
DJM DJS 302, May 1974

The Bitch Is Back/Cold Highway
DJM DJS 322, August 1974

Lucy In The Sky With Diamonds/One
Day At A Time
DJM DJS 340, November 1974

Philadelphia Freedom/I Saw Her
Standing There
DJM DJS 354, February 1975 (A-side
credited to the Elton John Band; B-side
to the Elton John Band featuring John
Lennon & the Muscle Shoals Horns)

Someone Saved My Life Tonight/House
Of Cards
DJM DJS 385, May 1975

Island Girl/Sugar On The Floor
DJM DJS 610, September 1975

Grow Some Funk Of Your Own/I Feel
Like A Bullet
DJM DJS 629, January 1976

Pinball Wizard/Harmony
DJM DJS 652, March 1976

Don't Go Breaking My Heart/Snow
Queen
Rocket ROKN 512, June 1976
(Duet with Kiki Dee)
Reissued on Rocket XPRESS 49, 1981

Bennie And The Jets/Rock And Roll
Madonna
DJM DJS 10705, September 1976

Sorry Seems To Be The Hardest
Word/Shoulder Holster
Rocket ROKN 517, October 1976

Crazy Water/Chameleon
Rocket ROKN 521, February 1977

The Goaldiggers Song
Rocket GOALD 1, March 1977
(Charity disc. Limited edition of 500
copies pressed)

Bite Your Lip/Chicago
Rocket ROKN 526, June 1977
(Double A-side. Chicago performed
only by Kiki Dee)

Four Eyes From Four Eyes EP: Your
Song/Rocket Man/Saturday Night's
Alright For Fighting/Whenever You're
Ready
DJM DJR 18001, 1977

Ego/Flintstone Boy
Rocket ROKN 538, March 1978

Part-Time Love/I Cry At Night
Rocket XPRESS 1, October 1978

Song For Guy/Lovesick
Rocket XPRESS 5, November 1978
Are You Ready For Love (Part 1)/Are
You Ready For Love (Part 2)Rocket
XPRESS 13, April 1979
(Other format also includes Three Way
Love Affair/Mama Can't Buy You Love)

Victim Of Love/Strangers
Rocket XPRESS 21, September 1979

Johnny B. Goode/Thunder In The Night
Rocket XPRESS 24, December 1979

Little Jeannie/Conquer The Sun
Rocket XPRESS 32, May 1980

Sartorial Eloquence/White Man
Danger/Cartier Commercial
Rocket XPRESS 41, August 1980

Dear God/Tactics
Rocket XPRESS 45, November 1980
(Other format also includes Steal Away
Child/Love So Cold)

I Saw Her Standing There/Whatever
Gets You Through The Night/Lucy In
The Sky With Diamonds
DJM DJS 10965, March 1981
(The Elton John Band featuring John
Lennon & the Muscle Shoals
Horns)

Nobody Wins/Fools In Fashion
Rocket XPRESS 54, May 1981

Loving You Is Sweeter Than Ever/
24 Hours (duet with Kiki Dee)
Ariola ARO 269, 1981

Just Like Belgium/Can't Get Over
Getting Over Losing You
Rocket XPRESS 59, July 1981

Blue Eyes/Hey Papa Legba
Rocket XPRESS 71, March 1982

Empty Garden/Take Me Down To The
Ocean
Rocket XPRESS 77, May 1982

Princess/The Retreat
Rocket XPRESS 85, September 1982

All Quiet On The Western Front/
Where Have All The Good Times
Gone?
Rocket XPRESS 88, November 1982

I Guess That's Why They Call It The
Blues/Choc Ice Goes Mental
Rocket XPRESS 91, April 1983
(B-side artist credit: Lord Choc Ice,
pseudonym for Elton John)

Les Aveux/Donner Pour Donner
(With France Gall)
Atlantic 11635, 1983

I'm Still Standing/Earn While You Learn
Rocket EJS 1, July 1983
(B-side artist credit: Lord Choc Ice,
pseudonym for Elton John)

Kiss The Bride/Dreamboat
Rocket EJS 2, October 1983
(Other format also includes Ego/Song
For Guy)

Cold As Christmas/Crystal
Rocket EJS 3, November 1983
(Other formats also include Don't Go
Breaking My Heart/Snow Queen
(duets with Kiki Dee) and J'veux d'la
Tendresse

Sad Songs/A Simple Man
Rocket PH 7, May 1984

Passengers/Lonely Boy
Rocket EJS 5, August 1984

Who Wears Those Shoes?/Tortured
Rocket EJS 6, October 1984
(Other format also includes I Heard It
Through The Grapevine [live])

Breaking Hearts/In Neon
Rocket EJS 7, February 1985

Act Of War (Part 1)/Act Of War
(Part 2)
Rocket EJS 8, June 1985
(duet with Millie Jackson)

Nikita/The Man Who Never Died
Rocket EJS 9, October 1985
(Other formats also include Sorry
Seems To Be The Hardest Word
live/I'm Still Standing [live])

Wrap Her Up/Restless live
Rocket EJS 10, November 1985
(A-side duet with George Michael)

Cry To Heaven/Candy By The Pound
Rocket EJS 11, February 1986
(Other format also includes Rock And
Roll Medley [live]: Whole
Lotta Shakin' Going On/I Saw Her
Standing There/Twist And Shout)

Heartache All Over The World/
Highlander
Rocket EJS, 12 September 1986

Slow Rivers/Billy And The Kids
Rocket EJS 13, November 1986
(A-side duet with Cliff Richard. Other
format also includes Lord Of The Flies)

Flames Of Paradise (Duet with Jennifer
Rush)/Call My Name
CBS 6508657, 1987

Your Song (Live)/Don't Let The Sun Go
Down On Me (Live)
Rocket EJS 14, July 1987
(Other format also includes I Need You
To Turn To [live]/The Greatest
Discovery [live])

Candle In The Wind (Live)/Sorry Seems
To Be The Hardest Word (Live)
Rocket EJS 15, January 1988
(Other formats also include Your Song
Live/Don't Let The Sun Go Down On
Me Live)

I Don't Wanna Go On With You Like
That/Rope Around A Fool
Rocket EJS 16, May 1988

Town Of Plenty/Whipping Boy
Rocket EJS 17, August 1988
(Other format also includes My Baby's
A Saint/I Guess That's Why They Call It
The Blues)

A Word In Spanish/Heavy Traffic
Rocket EJS 18, November 1988
(Other format also includes Song For
Guy/ Blue Eyes/ I Guess That's Why
They Call It The Blues

Healing Hands/Dancing In The End
Zone
Rocket EJS 19, August 1989
(Other formats also include Sad Songs)

Through The Storm (Duet with Aretha
Franklin)/Come To Me
Arista 112 185, 1989

Sacrifice/Love Is A Cannibal
Rocket EJS 20, October 1989

Sacrifice/Healing Hands
Rocket EJS 22, June 1990

Club At The End Of The Street/
Whispers
Rocket EJS 23, August 1990
(Other formats also include I Don't
Wanna Go On With You Like
That [live])

You Gotta Love Someone/Medicine
Man
Rocket EJS 24, October 1990

Easier To Walk Away/I Swear I Heard
The Night Talkin'
Rocket EJS 25, November 1990
(Other formats also include Made
For Me)

Don't Let The Sun Go Down On Me/
Song For Guy
Rocket EJS 26, February 1991
(Other formats also include Sorry
Seems To Be The Hardest Word)

Don't Let The Sun Go Down On Me/
I Believe
Epic 657646 7, November 1991
(A-side duet with George Michael/
B-side George Michael only)

The One/Suit Of Wolves
Rocket EJS 28, May 1992
(Other formats also include Your
Song/Don't Let The Sun Go Down
On Me/Sacrifice)

Runaway Train (with Eric Clapton)/
Understanding Women
Rocket EJS 29, August 1992
(Other formats also include Made
For Me)

The Last Song/The Man Who Never
Died
Rocket EJS 30, October 1992
(Other formats also include Song For
Guy/Are You Ready For Love/
Three Way Love Affair/Moma Can't
Buy You Love)

ORIGINAL ALBUMS

EMPTY SKY
Empty Sky/Val-Hala/Western Ford
Gateway/Hymn 2000/Lady, What's
Tomorrow?/Sails/The Scaffold/
Skyline Pigeon/Medley: Gulliver/Hay
Chewed.
DJM DJLPS 403, January 1969

ELTON JOHN
Your Song/I Need You To Turn To/
Take Me To The Pilot/No Shoe
Strings On Louise/First Episode At
Hienton/Sixty Years On/Border Song/
The Greatest Discovery/The Cage/
The King Must Die
DJM DJLPS 406, April 1970

TUMBLEWEED CONNECTION
Ballad Of A Well-Known Gun/Come
Down In Time/Country Comfort/Son
Of Your Father's/My Father's Gun/
Where To Now, St Peter?/Love
Song/Amoreena/Talking Old Soldiers/
Burn Down The Mission.
DJM DJLPS 410, October 1970

17-11-70
Take Me To The Pilot/Honky Tonk
Women/Sixty Years On/Can I Put
You On?/Bad Side Of The Moon/
Medley: Burn Down The Mission/My
Baby Left Me/Get Back
DJM DJLPS 414, April 1971

FRIENDS (ORIGINAL
SOUNDTRACK RECORDING)
Friends/Honey Roll/Variations on
Friends Theme (The First Kiss)/
Seasons/Variations on Michelle's Song
(A Day In The Country)/Can I Put You
On/Michelle's Song/I Meant To Do My
WorkToday/Four Moods/Seasons
(Reprise)
Paramount SPFL 269, April 1971

MADMAN ACROSS THE WATER
Tiny Dancer/Levon/Razor Face/
Madman Across The Water/Indian
Sunset/Holiday Inn/Rotten Peaches/All
The Nasties/Goodbye
DJM DJLPH 420, November 1971

HONKY CHÂTEAU
Honky Cat/Mellow/I Think I'm Going
To Kill Myself/Susie (Dramas)/Rocket
Man/Salvation/Slave/Amy/Mona Lisas
And Mad Hatters/Hercules
DJM DJLPH 423, May 1972

DON'T SHOOT ME, I'M ONLY THE
PIANO PLAYER
Daniel/Teacher, I Need You/Elderberry
Wine/Blues For My Baby And Me/
Midnight Creeper/Have Mercy On The
Criminal/I'm Going To Be A Teenage
Idol/Texan Love Song/Crocodile
Rock/High-Flying Bird
DJM DJLPH 427, January 1973

GOODBYE YELLOW BRICK ROAD
Medley: Funeral For A Friend/Love Lies
Bleeding/Candle In The Wind/Bennie
And The Jets/Goodbye Yellow Brick
Road/This Song Has No Title/Grey Seal/
Jamaica Jerk-Off/I've Seen That Movie
Too/Sweet Painted Lady/The Ballad Of
Danny Bailey (1909-34)/Dirty Little
Girl/All The Girls Love Alice/Your
Sister Can't Twist (But She Can Rock 'n'
Roll)/Saturday Night's Alright For
Fighting/Roy Rogers/Social Disease/
Harmony
DJM DJLPO 1001, October 1973
(Double LP)

CARIBOU
The Bitch Is Back/Pinky/Grimsby/Dixie
Lily/Solar Prestige A Gammon/You're
So Static/I've Seen The Saucers/
Stinker/Don't Let The Sun Go Down
On Me/Ticking
DJM DJLPS 439, June 1974

CAPTAIN FANTASTIC AND THE
BROWN DIRT COWBOY
Captain Fantastic And The Brown Dirt
Cowboy/Tower Of Babel/Bitter
Fingers/Tell Me When The Whistle
Blows/Someone Saved My Life Tonight/
(Gotta Get A) Meal Ticket/Better Off
Dead/Writing/We All Fall In Love
Sometimes/Curtains
DJM DJLPX 1, May 1975

ROCK OF THE WESTIES
Medley: Yell Help/Wednesday Night/
Ugly/Dan Dare (Pilot Of The Future)/
Island Girl/Grow Some Funk Of Your
Own/I Feel Like A Bullet (In The Gun Of
Robert Ford)/Street Kids/Hard Luck
Story/Feed Me/Billy Bones And The
White Bird
DJM DJLPH 464, October 1975

HERE AND THERE
(Side One - Live In London) Skyline
Pigeon/ Border Song/ Honky Cat/Love
Song/Crocodile Rock; (Side Two - Live
In New York) Funeral For A Friend/
Love Lies Bleeding/Rocket Man/Bennie
And The Jets/Take Me To The Pilot
DJM DJLPH 473, April 1976

BLUE MOVES
Your Starter For.../Tonight/One Horse
Town/Chameleon/Boogie Pilgrim/Cage
The Songbird/Crazy Water/Shoulder
Holster/Sorry Seems To Be The
Hardest Word/Out Of The Blue/
Between Seventeen And Twenty/The
Wide-Eyed And Laughing/Someone's
Final Song/-Where's The Shoorah?/If
There's A God In Heaven (What's He
Waiting For?)/Idol/Theme From A
Non-Existent TV Series/Bite Your Lip
(Get Up And Dance)
Rocket ROSP 1, October 1976
(Double LP)

A SINGLE MAN
Shine On Through/Return To Paradise/
I Don't Care/Big Dipper/It Ain't Gonna
Be Easy/Part-Time Love/Georgia/
Shooting Star/Madness/ Reverie/Song
For Guy
Rocket TRAIN 1, October 1978

VICTIM OF LOVE
Johnny B. Goode/Warm Love In A Cold
World/Born Bad/Thunder In The
Night/Spotlight/Street Boogie/Victim
Of Love
Rocket HISPD 124, October 1979

21 AT 33
Chasing The Crown/Little Jeannie/
Sartorial Eloquence/Two Rooms AtThe
End Of The World/White Lady White
Power/Dear God/Never Gonna Fall In
Love Again/Take Me Back/Give Me The
Love
Rocket HISPD 126, May 1980

THE FOX
Breaking Down The Barriers/Heart In
The Right Place/Just Like Belgium/
Nobody Wins/Fascist Faces/Medley:
Carla, Etude, Fanfare, Chloe/Heels Of
The Wind/Elton's Song/The Fox
Rocket TRAIN 16, May 1981

JUMP UP!
Dear John/Spiteful Child/Ball &
Chain/Legal Boys/I Am Your Robot/
Blue Eyes/Empty Garden (Hey Hey
Johnny)/Princess/Where Have All The
Good Times Gone?/All Quiet On The
Western Front
Rocket HISPD 127, April 1982

TOO LOW FOR ZERO
Cold As Christmas/I'm Still
Standing/Too Low For Zero/Religion/
I Guess That's Why They Call It The
Blues/Crystal/Kiss The Bride/Whipping
Boy/My Baby's A Saint/One More
Arrow
Rocket HISPD 24, June 1983

BREAKING HEARTS
Restless/Slow Down Georgie (She's
Poison)/Who Wears These Shoes?/
Breaking Hearts (Ain't What It Used To
Be)/Li'l 'Frigerator/ Passengers/In Neon/
Burning Buildings/Did He Shoot Her?/
Sad Songs (Say So Much)
Rocket HISPD 25, June 1984

ICE ON FIRE
This Town/Cry To Heaven/Soul
Glove/Nikita/Too Young/Wrap Her
Up/Satellite/Tell Me What The Papers
Say/Candy By The Pound/Shoot Down
The Moon
Rocket HISPD 26, November 1985

LEATHER JACKETS
Leather Jackets/Hoop Of Fire/Don't
Trust That Woman/Go It Alone/Gypsy
Heart/Slow Rivers/Heartache All Over
The World/Angeline/Memory Of
Love/Paris/I Fall Apart
Rocket EJLP 1, November 1986

LIVE IN AUSTRALIA
Sixty Years On/I Need You To Turn
To/The Greatest Discovery/Tonight/
Sorry Seems To Be The Hardest Word/
The King Must Die/Take Me To The
Pilot/Tiny Dancer/Have Mercy On The
Criminal/Madman Across The Water/
Candle In The Wind/Burn Down The
Mission/Your Song/Don't Let The Sun
Go Down On Me
Rocket EJBXL 1, September 1987
(Double LP)

REG STRIKES BACK
Town Of Plenty/A Word In
Spanish/Mona Lisas And Mad Hatters
(Part Two)/I Don't Want To Go On
With You Like That/Japanese Hands/
Goodbye Marlon Brando/The Camera
Never Lies/Heavy Traffic/Poor Cow/
Since God Invented Girls
Rocket EJLP 3, July 1988

SLEEPING WITH THE PAST
Durban Deep/Healing Hands/
Whispers/Club At The End Of The
Street/ Sleeping With The Past/Stones
Throw From Hurin'/Sacrifice/I Never
Knew Her Name/Amazes Me/Blue
Avenue
Rocket 838 839 1, September 1989

THE ONE
Simple Life/The One/Sweat It Out/
Runaway Train/Whitewash County/
The North/When A Woman Doesn't
Want You/Emily/On Dark Street/
Understanding Women/The Last Song
Rocket 512 360-1, June 1992

ALBUM PRODUCTION WORK & GUEST APPEARANCES

I WHO HAVE NOTHING - Tom Jones
Decca SKL 5072, April 1970
Contributed backing vocals on
Daughter Of Darkness

CONFESSIONS OF THE MIND - The Hollies
Parlophone PC 5 7117, November 1970
Contributed piano on Perfect Lady Housewife

SING CHILDREN SING -Lesley Duncan
June 1971
Contributed piano to one or more unspecified tracks

IT AIN'T EASY - John Baldry
Warner Bros K 46088 July 1971
Produced and contributed piano to Side Two

SMILING FACE - Davey Johnstone
Rocket, May 1973
Played harmonium on Keep Right On

LOVING AND FREE - Kiki Dee
Rocket ROLL 5, December 1973
Co-produced all tracks (with Clive Franks)

FOR EVERYMAN - Jackson Browne
January 1974
Contributed piano on Redneck Friend

SMILER - Rod Stewart
Mercury 9104 001, September 1974
Contributed piano and vocals on Let Me Be Your Car

WALLS AND BRIDGES - John Lennon
Parlophone PCTC 245, October 1974
Contributed piano, organ and backing vocals on Whatever Gets You Through The Night and Surprise Surprise

GOODNIGHT VIENNA - Ringo Starr
Apple PMC 7168, November 1974
Contributed piano on Snookeroo

OVERNIGHT SUCCESS - Neil Sedaka
February 1975
Sang harmony vocal on Bad Blood

TOMMY - Original Soundtrack Recording
Track/Polydor 2657002, March 1975
Pinball Wizard

SWEET DECEIVER - Kevin Ayers
March 1975
Contributed piano on Circular Letter

NIGEL OLSSON - Nigel Olsson
Rocket, November 1975
Played keyboards on Only One Woman

WORD CALLED LOVE - Brian and Brenda Russell
Rocket, June 1976
Contributed piano and backing vocals on Tell Me When The Whistle Blows

STEPPIN' OUT - Neil Sedaka
Rocket, June 1976

KIKI DEE - Kiki Dee
Rocket ROLA 3, March 1977
Co-produced all tracks (with Clive Franks)

ANOTHER NIGHT TIME FLIGHT - Blue
Rocket, June 1977
Co-produced all tracks (with Clive Franks)

CHINA - China
Rocket ROLL 9, October 1977
Produced all tracks (with Clive Franks and China)

PUTTIN' ON THE STYLE - Lonnie Donegan
Chrysalis CHR 1158, January 1978
Contributed piano on Diggin' My Potatoes and Puttin' On The Style

PERFECT TIMING - Kiki Dee
Ariola ARL 5050, June 1981
Sang duet with Kiki Dee on Loving You Is Sweeter Than Ever

FRIENDS - Dionne Warwick
Arista 207438, December 1985
Contributed backing vocals with Stevie Wonder and Gladys Knight on That's What Friends Are For

ROCK THE NATIONS - Saxon
EMI EMC 3515, September 1986
Contributed piano on Northern Lady

HEART OVER MIND - Jennifer Rush
CBS 450 4701, April 1987
Sang duet with Jennifer Rush on Flames Of Paradise

THE PRINCE'S TRUST 10TH ANNIVERSARY BIRTHDAY PARTY - Various Artists
A & M, April 1987
I'm Still Standing (live)
Also played piano in the all-star band backing guest vocalists

THE PRINCE'S TRUST CONCERT 1987 - Various Artists
A & M AMA 3906 & PTA 1987, August 1987
Saturday Night's Alright For Fighting/ Your Song (live)
Also played piano in all-star band backing guest vocalists

CLOUD NINE - George Harrison
Dark Horse WX 123, November 1987
Contributed piano on Devil's Radio and Wreck Of The Hesperus and electric piano on title track

25 YEARS OF ROCK 'N ROLL 1972 - Various Artists
Connoisseur Collection YRNRCD72, 1988
Rocket Man

25 YEARS OF ROCK 'N ROLL 1973 - Various Artists
Connoisseur Collection YRNRCD73, 1988
Goodbye Yellow Brick Road

25 YEARS OF ROCK 'N ROLL 1974 - Various Artists
Connoisseur Collection YRNRCD74, 1988
Candle In The Wind

NOW THAT'S WHAT I CALL MUSIC 12 - Various Artists
EMI CDNOW12, July 1988
I Don't Want To Go On With You Like That

THE RUMOUR - Olivia Newton-John
Mercury 834 957-1, October 1988
Co-produced and contributed digital piano and vocals on title track.

21 YEARS OF ALTERNATIVE RADIO 1 - Various Artists
BBC Records, October 1988
My Father's Gun (A BBC Radio session recording made in 1970)

ROCK RHYTHM & BLUES - Various Artists
Warner Brothers WX 255, May 1989
I'm Ready (new exclusive cover version recording)

HEARTBEATS - Various Artists
Masterpiece STDCD24, June 1989
Don't Let The Sun Go Down On Me

GHOSTBUSTERS II - Original Soundtrack Recording
MCA MCG 6056, July 1989
Love Is A Cannibal

MILESTONES: 20 ROCK OPERAS
Telstar TCD 2379, December 1989
Don't Let The Sun Go Down On Me

NOBODY'S CHILD (Rumanian Angel Appeal Charity Album)- Various Artists
WEA WX353, July 1990
Medicine Man

THE BLAZE OF GLORY: YOUNG GUNS II - Jon Bon Jovi
Vertigo 846 4731, August 1990
Contributed piano on Billy Get Your Guns and piano and backing vocals on Dyin' Ain't Much Of A Livin'

KNEBWORTH: THE ALBUM - Various Artists
Polydor 8439211, August 1990
Sad Songs/Saturday Night's Alright For Fighting (live)

UNDER THE RED SKY - Bob Dylan
CBS 4671881, September 1990
Contributed piano on 2 x 2

DAYS OF THUNDER - Original Soundtrack Recording
DGC 467 159, 1990
You Gotta Love Someone

MUSIC FROM THE FILM ROCKY V - Original Soundtrack Recording
Capitol EST 2137, January 1991
The Measure Of A Man

FREE - Rick Astley
RCA PL 74896, February 1991
Contributed piano on Behind The Smile and Wonderful You

MODERN LOVE - Various Artists
Polygram TV 5155181, June 1992
Don't Let The Sun Go Down On Me (Duet with George Michael)

FERN GULLY - Original Soundtrack Recording
MCA, 1992
Some Other World

COMPILATIONS

GREATEST HITS
Your Song/Daniel/Honky Cat/Goodbye Yellow Brick Road/Saturday Night's Alright For Fighting/Rocket Man/Candle In The Wind/Don't Let The Sun Go Down On Me/Border Song/Crocodile Rock
DJM DJLPH 422, November 1974

HERE AND THERE
Skyline Pigeon/Border Song/Honky Cat/Love Song/Crocodile Rock/ Medley: Funeral For A Friend/Love Lies Bleeding/Rocket Man/Bennie And The Jets/Take Me To The Pilot
DJM DJLPH 473, April 1976

GREATEST HITS VOLUME II
The Bitch Is Back/Lucy In The Sky With Diamonds/Sorry Seems To Be The Hardest Word/Don't Go Breaking My Heart/Someone Saved My Life Tonight/ Philadelphia Freedom/Island Girl/Grow Some Funk Of Your Own/Bennie & The Jets/Pinball Wizard
DJM DJLPH 20520, September 1977

CANDLE IN THE WIND
Skyline Pigeon/Take Me To The Pilot/ Burn Down The Mission/Teacher I Need You/Rocket Man/Don't Let The Sun Go Down On Me/Elderberry Wine/ Bennie & The Jets/Midnight Creeper/ Dan Dare/Someone Saved My Life Tonight/Better Off Dead/Grey Seal/ Candle In The Wind
St Michael 2094/0102, January 1978
(This album was released by CBS Special Products for the Marks and Spencer chain stores)

LONDON AND NEW YORK
Rocket Man/Crocodile Rock/Bennie And The Jets/Funeral For A Friend/Take Me To The Pilot/Skyline Pigeon/Honky Cat
Hallmark SHM 942, January 1978

ELTON JOHN LIVE COLLECTION
Take Me To The Pilot/Honky Tonk Women/Sixty Years On/Can I Put You On?/Skyline Pigeon/Border Song/Honky Cat/Love Song/Crocodile Rock/Bad Side Of The Moon/Burn Down The Mission/Funeral For A Friend/Love Lies Bleeding/Rocket Man/Bennie And The Jets
Pickwick PDA 047, January 1979

THE ELTON YEARS
Lady Samantha/Skyline Pigeon/Empty Sky/Border Song/I Need You To Turn To/Sixty Years On/Country Comfort/Burn Down The Mission/Where To Now St Peter/Levon/Madman Across The Water/Friends/Saturday Night's Alright For Fighting/(Gotta Get A) Meal Ticket/ Screw You/Teacher I Need You/Grow Some Funk Of Your Own/Grey Seal/The Bitch Is Back/Crocodile Rock/The Cage/Elderberry Wine/Whenever You're Ready/Street Kids/Midnight Creeper/Pinball Wizard/I Feel Like A Bullet/Mona Lisas & Mad Hatters/High Flying Bird/Tiny Dancer/The Greatest Discovery/Blues For My Baby & Me/Harmony/I've Seen That Movie Too/Pinky/It's Me That You Need/Indian Sunset/Sweet Painted Lady/Love Song/Your Song/Rocket Man/Honky Cat/Daniel/Goodbye Yellow Brick Road/Candle In The Wind/Don't Let The Sun Go Down On Me/Lucy In The Sky With Diamonds/Philadelphia Freedom/Someone Saved My Life Tonight/Island Girl/Bennie & The Jets/Funeral For A Friend/Love Lies Bleeding/The Ballad Of Danny Bailey 1909-34/Ticking/Texan Love Song/Captain Fantastic & The Brown Dirt Cowboy/We All Fall In Love Sometimes/Curtains
DJM LSP 14512, August 1979
(5 LP boxed set released for mail order only)

THE VERY BEST OF ELTON JOHN
Your Song/Goodbye Yellow Brick Road/Daniel/Song For Guy/Candle In The Wind/Friends/Tiny Dancer/Rocket Man/Don't Go Breaking My Heart/Sorry Seems To Be The Hardest Word/Border Song/Someone Saved My Life Tonight/Mona Lisas & Mad Hatters/Harmony/High Flying Bird/Don't Let The Sun Go Down On Me
K-Tel NE 1094, October 1980

LADY SAMANTHA
Rock & Roll Madonna/Whenever You're Ready/Bad Side Of The Moon/Jack Rabbit/Into The Old Man's Shoes/It's Me That You Need/Ho!Ho!Ho I Who'd Be A Turkey At Christmas/Skyline Pigeon/Screw You/Just Like Strange Rain/Grey Seal/The Honey Roll/Lady Samantha/Friends
DJM 22085, October 1980

THE ALBUM
Goodbye Yellow Brick Road/Burn Down The Mission/Sixty Years On/Crocodile Rock/Lucy In The Sky With Diamonds/Rock And Roll Madonna/Country Comfort/Harmony/Sweet Painted Lady/Pinball Wizard/Skyline Pigeon/Lady Samantha
Hallmark SHM 3088, September 1981

GREATEST HITS
Your Song/Daniel/Honky Cat/Goodbye Yellow Brick Road/Saturday Night's Alright For Fighting/Rocket Man/Candle In The Wind/Don't Let The Sun Go Down On Me/Border Song/Crocodile Rock/The Bitch Is Back/Lucy In The Sky With Diamonds/Sorry Seems To Be The Hardest Word/Don't Go Breaking My Heart/Someone Saved My Life Tonight/Philadelphia Freedom/

Island Girl/Grow Some Funk Of Your Own/Bennie And The Jets/Pinball Wizard
DJM DJLP 1, December 1981
(Double LP)

LOVE SONGS
Blue Eyes/Little Jeannie/Sartorial Eloquence/Chloe/Song For Guy/Shine On Through/Elton's Song/Tonight/Sorry Seems To Be The Hardest Word/All Quiet On The Western Front/Princess/Chameleon/ Return To Paradise/Someone's Final Love Song/Strangers/Never Gonna Fall In Love Again
TV Records TVA 3, February 1984

THE NEW COLLECTION
Crocodile Rock/Don't Let The Sun Go Down On Me/Saturday Night's Alright For Fighting/It's Me That You Need/Someone Saved My Life Tonight/Whatever Gets You Through The Night/Lucy In The Sky With Diamonds/The Bitch Is Back/High Flying Bird/Elderberry Wine/Candle In The Wind/Your Sister Can't Twist/Daniel
Premier CBR 1027, April 1984

THE NEW COLLECTION VOL 2
Premier CBR 1036, May 1984

SEASONS: THE EARLY LOVE SONGS
Amoreena/Amy/Writing/Curtains/Mellow/Empty Sky/Susie/Sails/ Goodbye/Come Down In Time/Sweet Painted Lady/Candle In The Wind/Funeral For A Friend/It's Me That You Need/We All Fall In Love Sometimes
Cambra CR 130, May 1984
(Double LP)

ELTON JOHN - THE COLLECTION
Funeral For A Friend/Love Lies Bleeding/Sweet Painted Lady/Elderberry Wine/Come Down In Time/I Need You To Turn To/Border Song/Crocodile Rock/Mona Lisas And The Hatters/The Greatest Discovery/Country Comfort/Blues For My Baby And Me/Harmony/Teacher I Need You/Ballad Of A Well Known Gun
Pickwick PWKS551, June 1989

THE VERY BEST OF ELTON JOHN
Your Song/Rocket Man/Honky Cat/Crocodile Rock/Daniel/Goodbye Yellow Brick Road/Saturday Night's Alright For Fighting/Candle In The Wind/Don't Let The Sun Go Down On Me/Lucy In The Sky With Diamonds/Philadelphia Freedom/Someone Saved My Life Tonight/Pinball Wizard/The Bitch Is Back/Don't Go Breaking My Heart/Bennie And The Jets/Sorry Seems To Be The Hardest Word/Song For Guy/Part Time Love/Blue Eyes/I Guess That's Why They Call It The Blues/I'm Still Standing/Kiss The Bride/Sad Songs/Passengers/Nikita/I Don't Wanna Go On With You Like That/Sacrifice/Easier To Walk Away/You Gotta Love Someone
Rocket 846 947-1, October 1990
(Double LP)

COMPACT DISC SINGLES

I Don't Want To Go On With You Like That/I Don't Want To Go On With You Like That (Shep Pettibone mix)
Rocket EJSCD 16, May 1988

Town Of Plenty/Whipping Boy/My Baby's A Saint/I Guess That's Why They Call It The Blues
Rocket EJSCD 17, August 1988

A Word In Spanish/Heavy Traffic/Medley: Song For You, Blue Eyes, I Guess That's Why They Call It The Blues (live)/Daniel
Rocket EJSCD 18, November 1988

Healing Hands/Dancing In The End Zone/Sad Songs
Rocket EJCD 19, August 1989

Club At The End Of The Street/Give Peace A Chance/I Don't Want To Go On With You Like That
Rocket EJSCD 21, July 1990

Sacrifice/Love Is A Cannibal
Rocket EJSCD 22, October 1990

You Gotta Love Someone/Medicine Man/Medicine Man (with Adamski)
Rocket EJS CD 24, October 1990

Easier To Walk Away/I Swear I Heard The Night Talking/Made For Me
Rocket EJSCD 25, November 1990

Don't Let The Sun Go Down On Me/Song For Guy/Sorry Seems To Be The Hardest Word
Rocket EJSCD 26, February 1991

The One/Your Song/Don't Let The Sun Go Down On Me/Sacrifice
Rocket EJSCR 28, May 1992

Runaway Train (with Eric Clapton)/Understanding Women/Made For Me
Rocket EJSCD 29, September 1992

ORIGINAL ALBUMS ON CD

21 AT 33
Rocket 800 055-2, 1983

TOO LOW FOR ZERO
Rocket 811 052-2, 1983

CAPTAIN FANTASTIC & THE BROWN DIRT COWBOY
DJM CD 1, November 1983 & DJM 821 746 2, November 1987

JUMP UP
Rocket 800 037-2, November 1983

BREAKING HEARTS
Rocket 822 088-2, June 1984

THE FOX
Rocket 800 063-2, July 1984

GOODBYE YELLOW BRICK ROAD
DJM 821 747-2, October 1984

ICE ON FIRE
Rocket 826 213-2, November 1985

A SINGLE MAN
Rocket 826 805 2, June 1986

TUMBLEWEED CONNECTION
DJM 829 248-2, June 1986

LEATHER JACKETS
Rocket 830 487-2, November 1986

LIVE IN AUSTRALIA
Rocket 832 470-2, February 1987 (Boxed Set) and August 1987 (Standard Format)

EMPTY SKY
DJM, April 1987

HONKY CHÂTEAU
DJM 829 249-2, June 1987

LADY SAMANTHA
DJM 823 019-2, June 1987

MADMAN ACROSS THE WATER
DJM 825 487-2, June 1987

ELTON JOHN
DJM 827 689 2, June 1987 & CD 8, 1988

CARIBOU
DJM CD 6, November 1987

DON'T SHOOT ME, I'M ONLY THE PIANO PLAYER
DJM CD 10, November 1987

ROCK OF THE WESTIES
DJM CD 9, November 1987

REG STRIKES BACK
Rocket 834 701 2, July 1988

BLUE MOVES
Rocket 822 818-2, June 1989

SLEEPING WITH THE PAST
Rocket 838 839-2, September 1989

TO BE CONTINUED
Rocket 848 236-2, November 1991

THE ONE
Rocket 512 360-2, June 1992

COMPILATIONS ON COMPACT DISC

LOVE SONGS
Rocket 814 085-2, February 1984

GREATEST HITS VOL 1
DJM CD 3, October 1984

SUPERIOR SOUND OF ELTON JOHN 1970-1975
Your Song/Crocodile Rock/Rocket Man/Daniel/Saturday Night's Alright For Fighting/Goodbye Yellow Brick Road/Funeral For A Friend/Love Lies Bleeding/Don't Let The Sun Go Down On Me/Philadelphia Freedom/Someone Saved My Life Tonight/We All Fall In Love Sometimes
DJM CD 4, October 1984 (CD Only)

GREATEST HITS VOL 2
DJM CD 7, October 1985

THE ELTON JOHN COLLECTION
Pickwick PWKS 551, October 1989

THE VERY BEST OF ELTON JOHN
Rocket 846 917-2, October 1990

IMPORTANT OVERSEAS RELEASES

SINGLES

From Denver To LA
Viking VIK 1010, April 1970: USA
A-side not released in UK

Les Aveux/Donner Pour Donner
Atlantic ATL 11 635, February 1981:
France A & B sides not released in UK
(Duets with France Gall)

Chloe/Troubled
July 1981: USA
B-side not released in UK

ALBUMS

THE GAMES - Original Soundtrack Recording
Viking LPS 105, April 1970: USA
From Denver To LA
Not released in UK

THE COMPLETE THOM BELL SESSIONS
MCA 39115, February 1989: USA
Mama Can't Buy You Love/Are You Ready For Love/Three Way Love Affair/Nice And Slow*/Country Love Song*/Shine On Through*
* Denotes previously unreleased material.
Not released in UK

TO BE CONTINUED
(Four CD/Cassette Box Set)
MCA 10110, October 1990: USA
Come Back Baby (the début Bluesology single)/Lady Samantha/It's Me That You Need/Your Song(solo demo version)/Rock And Roll Madonna/Bad Side Of The Moon/Your Song/Take Me To The Pilot/Border Song/Sixty Years On/Country Comfort/Grey Seal(original 1970 version)/Friends/Levon/Tiny Dancer/Madman Across The Water/Honky Cat/Mona Lisas And Mad Hatters/Rocket Man/Daniel/Crocodile Rock/Bennie And The Jets/Goodbye Yellow Brick Road/All The Girls Love Alice/Funeral For A Friend/Love Lies Bleeding/Whenever You're Ready/Saturday Night's Alright For Fighting/Jack Rabbit/Harmony/Young Man's Blues/Step Into Christmas/The Bitch Is Back/Pinball Wizard/Someone Saved My Life Tonight/Philadelphia Freedom/One Day At A Time/Lucy In The Sky With Diamonds/I Saw Her Standing There/Island Girl/Sorry Seems To Be The Hardest Word/Don't Go Breaking My Heart/I Feel Like A Bullet (new 1990 version)/Ego/Song For Guy/Mama Can't Buy You Love/Cartier Commercial/Little Jeannie/Donner Pour Donner/Fanfare/Chloe/The Retreat/Blue Eyes/Empty Garden/I Guess That's Why They Call It The Blues/I'm Still Standing/Sad Songs/Act Of War/Nikita/Candle In The Wind/Carla Etude(live version)/Don't Let The Sun Go Down On Me/I Don't Want To Go On With You Like That/Give Peace A Chance/Sacrifice/Made For Me(new 1990 version)/You Gotta Love Someone/I Swear I Heard The Night Talking(new 1990 version)/Easier To Walk Away(new 1990 version)
Not released in UK

FOR OUR CHILDREN -
Various Artists
May 1991: USA
Paediatric AIDS Foundation charity album for which Elton contributed a recording of The Pacifier
Not released in UK

BOOKS

ELTON JOHN
Dick Tatham & Tony Jasper
(Octopus, 1976)

ELTON JOHN - THE ILLUSTRATED DISCOGRAPHY
Alan Finch (Omnibus Press, 1981)

ELTON JOHN
Chris Charlesworth (Bobcat, 1986)

ELTON JOHN - A BIOGRAPHY
Barry Toberman (Weidenfeld & Nicolson, 1988)

ELTON
Philip Norman (Hutchinson, 1991)

TWO ROOMS
A collection of interviews compiled by Lorna Dickson & Claudia Rosencrantz (Boxtree Publishing, 1991)

VIDEOS

THE FOX
Breaking Down the Barriers/Heart In The Right Place/Just Like Belgium/Nobody Wins/Fascist Faces/Carla Etude/Fanfare/Chloe/Heels Of The Wind/The Fox
Rank Video, 1981

THE VIDEO SINGLES
I Guess That's Why They Call It The Blues/Empty Garden/I'm Still Standing/Blue Eyes
Polygram Video, 1983

ELTON JOHN STORY
All The Young Girls Love Alice/Goodbye Yellow Brick Road/Ballad Of Danny Bailey/Candle In The Wind/Rocket Man/Funeral For A Friend/Saturday Night's Alright For Fighting
Orion Communications

LIVE IN CENTRAL PARK - NEW YORK
Saturday Night's Alright For Fighting/Little Jeannie/Benny And The Jets/Imagine/Someone Saved My Life Tonight/Goodbye Yellow Brick Road/Sorry Seems To Be The Hardest Word/Your Song/Bite Your Lip
VCL, September 1986

TO RUSSIA WITH ELTON
Strolling In The Park/Crocodile Rock/Pinball Wizard/Saturday Night's Alright For Fighting/Piano Concerto/Back In The USSR/Get Back/Back In The USSR/Internationale/Your Song/Daniel/Funeral For A Friend/Tonight/Part Time Love/Strolling In The Par/Bennie And The Jets/Midnight In Moscow/Russian Rock & Roll Song/60 Years On/Candle In The Wind/Better Off Dead/Rocket Man/Think I'm Gonna Kill Myself/Saturday Night's Alright For Fighting/Pinball Wizard/SaturdayNight's All Right For Fighting.
Channel 5, December 1986

AFTERNOON CONCERT
Hercules/Rocket Man/Daniel/Restless/Candle In The Wind/The Bitch Is Back/Don't Let The Sun Go Down On Me/Sad Songs/Bennie & The Jets
Vestron, December 1986

NIGHT TIME CONCERT
Sorry Seems To Be The Hardest Word/I Guess That's Why They Call It The Blues/Your Song/Saturday Night's Alright For Fighting/Goodbye Yellow Brick Road/Too Low For Zero/Kiss The Bride/I'm Still Standing/Whole Lotta Shakin' Goin' On/I Saw Her Standing There/Twist And Shout
Vestron, December 1986

THE VIDEO SINGLES
Channel 5, April 1987

LIVE IN AUSTRALIA 1: SYDNEY ENTERTAINMENT CENTRE 14 DECEMBER 1986
Funeral For A Friend/One Horse Town/Rocket Man/The Bitch Is Back/Daniel/Medley: Song For You/Blue Eyes/I Guess That's Why They Call It The Blues/Bennie And The Jets/Sad Songs/I'm Still Standing
Virgin, May 1987

LIVE IN AUSTRALIA 2: SYDNEY ENTERTAINMENT CENTRE 14 DECEMBER 1986
60 Years On/I Need You To Turn To/Greatest Discovery/Sorry Seems To Be The Hardest Word/Take Me To The Pilot/Have Mercy On A Criminal/Don't Let The Sun Go Down On Me/Candle In The Wind/Burn Down The Mission/Your Song/Saturday Night's Alright For Fighting
Virgin, May 1987

THE VERY BEST OF ELTON JOHN
Your Song/Daniel/Goodbye Yellow Brick Road/Don't Go Breaking My Heart/Sorry Seems To Be The Hardest Word/Rocket Man/Blue Eyes/I Guess That's Why They Call It The Blues/I'm Still Standing/Kiss The Bride/Sad Songs Say So Much/Passengers/Nikita/Wrap Her Up/Candle In Wind/The Saturday Night's Alright For Fighting/I Don't Wanna Go On With You Like That/Philadelphia Freedom/Sacrifice/You Gotta Love Someone
Channel 5, October 1990

LIVE IN BARCELONA
Don't Let The Sun Go Down On Me/I'm Still Standing/I Guess That's Why They Call It The Blues/Tiny Dancer/Philadelphia Freedom/Burn Down The Mission/Simple Life/The One/Mona Lisa And Mad Hatters/Sorry Seems To Be The Hardest Word/Daniel/Blue Avenue/Last Song/Funeral For A Friend/Show Must Go On/Saturday Nights Alright For Fighting/Sacrifice/Song For Guy
Music Vision, September 1992

PROMOTIONAL VIDEOS

Your Song (1971)
Daniel (1973)
Goodbye Yellow Brick Road (1973)
Don't Go Breaking My Heart (1976)
Sorry Seems To Be The Hardest Word (1976)
Rocket Man (1977)
Blue Eyes (1982)
I Guess That's Why They Call It The Blues (1983)
I'm Still Standing (1983)
Kiss The Bride (1983)
Sad Songs Say So Much (1984)
Passengers (1984)
Nikita (1985)
Wrap Her Up (1985)
Candle In The Wind (1986)
Saturday Night's Alright For Fighting (1987)
I Don't Wanna Go On With You Like That (1988)
Philadelphia Freedom (1989)
Sacrifice (1989)
You Gotta Love Someone (1990)
Club At The End Of The Street (1990)
The One (1992)

SELECTED BOOTLEGS

ALL ACROSS THE HAVENS
(LIVE RECORDING OF ODEON HAMMERSMITH CONCERT: 24 DECEMBER 1974)
Funeral For A Friend/Love Lies Bleeding/Candle In The Wind/Grimsby/Crocodile Rock/Goodbye Yellow Brick Road/Grey Seal/Don't Let The Sun Go Down On Me/Saturday Night's Alright For Fighting/Your Song
TAKRL 1946.

I GET A LITTLE BIT LONELY
(A COLLECTION OF STUDIO DEMOS: 1968-1970)
I Get A Little Bit Lonely/The Flowers Will Never Die/Rock Me When He's Gone/Tartan Coloured Lady/I've Been Loving You/Sitting Doing Nothing/Sing Me No Sad Songs/I Love You & That's All That Matters/The Tide Will Turn For Rebecca/A Dandelion Dies In The Wind/Hourglass/Baby I Miss You/Reminds Me Of You/When The First Tear Shows
Appy Records APPY 1/2

THE BITCH IS BACK
(DIRECT PIRATE OF CARIBOU OFFICIAL RELEASE)
The Bitch Is Back/Pinky/Grimsby/Dixie Lily/Solar Prestige Gammon/You're So Static/I've Seen The Saucers/Stinker/Don't Let The Sun Go Down On Me/Ticking
WPLJ1.

ELTON IN DISGUISE WITH GLASSES
(LIVE RECORDING OF THE FORUM INGLEWOOD CALIFORNIA CONCERT: 5 OCTOBER 1974)
Grimsby/Rocket Man/Take Me To The Pilot/Bennie And The Jets/Grey Seal/Daniel/You're So Static/Lucy In The Sky With Diamonds/Don't Let The Sun Go Down On Me/Honky Cat
Phonygraf P1113.

JUST LIKE STRANGE RAIN
(LIVE RECORDING OF ODEON HAMMERSMITH CONCERT: 24 DECEMBER 1974)
Rocket Man/High Flying Bird/Burn Down The Mission/The Bitch Is Back/

Daniel/Bennie & The Jets/Lucy In The Sky With Diamonds/I Saw Her Standing There/Honky Cat The Amazing Kornyphone Label TAKRL 1974.

KNOCKING 'EM DEAD ALIVE
(FM RECORDING OF LIVE CONCERT BROADCAST BY WABC NEW YORK: 17 NOVEMBER 1970)
I Need You To Turn To/Your Song/Far Side Of The Moon/Country Comfort/Can I Put You Off/Border Song/Sixty Years On/Indian Sunset/Honky Tonk Women/Amoreena/Take Me To The Pilot/Burn Down The Mission/Medley including Get Back/My Baby Left Me/My Father's Gun.
Kustom Records KR 2006.

LIVE IN LONDON
(LIVE RECORDING OF THE CRYSTAL PALACE GARDEN PARTY CONCERT: 31 JULY 1971)
Skyline Pigeon/Rock Me When He's Gone/I Need You To Turn To/Tiny Dancer/Love Song/Razor Face/Indian Sunset/Whole Lotta Shakin'
The Strait Record Co STR 001.

LIVE AT THE STADIUM
(LIVE RECORDING OF THE WEMBLEY STADIUM CONCERT: 21 JUNE 1975)
Captain Fantastic & The Brown Dirt Cowboy/Meal Ticket/Better Off Dead/Tell Me When The Whistle Blows/Someone Saved My Life Tonight/We All Fall In Love Some Time/Curtains
WEM 1/2.

OPENING NIGHT
(LIVE RECORDING OF LOS ANGELES UNIVERSAL AMPHITHEATER CONCERT: 26 SEPTEMBER 1979)
I Heard It Through The Grapevine/I Feel Like A Bullet/Bennie And The Jets/Tonight/Better Off Dead/Idol/I Think I'm Gonna Kill Myself

SUPERSTAR LIVE
(A COLLECTION OF RECORDINGS TAKEN FROM VARIOUS LIVE CONCERTS: 1970)
I Need You To Turn To/Your Song/Bad Side Of The Moon/Country Comfort/Border Song/60 Years On/Honky Tonk Women/Amareena
EJL 501.

WEST OF THE ROCKIES
(LIVE RECORDING OF DODGER STADIUM LOS ANGELES CONCERT: 25 OCTOBER 1975 & SAN DIEGO CALIFORNIA CONCERT: 29 AUGUST 1975)
Your Song/Lucy In The Sky With Diamonds/I Saw Her Standing There/Island Girl/Harmony/Pinball Wizard/Captain Fantastic & The Brown Dirt Cowboy/Someone Saved My Life Tonight/Don't Let The Sun Go Down On Me
Impossible Records IMP 1104.